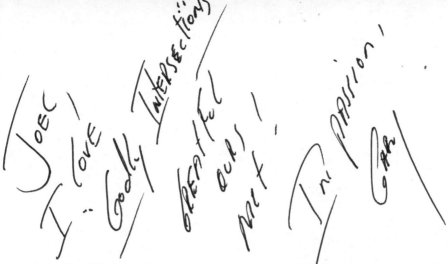

Joel — I love ... "Godly Intersections" Heartful ours pact! True Passion! Gary

The Passion-Centered Person

How to Go From Having Just a Career to Having a Life

Gary Zelesky

with Tim Vandehey

LiveMic Publications

Printed in the United States of America.

For information address:
LiveMic Publications
5665 Kingswood Dr, Citrus Heights, CA 95610

Library of Congress Cataloging-in-Publication Data
Zelesky, Gary, 1952 -

The Passion-Centered Person / Gary Zelesky

Library of Congress Control Number: 2007929256

p. cm.

ISBN: 978-0-9834079-3-5

Third Edition

10 9 8 7 6 5 4 3 2 1

Visit our Web site at
www.GaryZelesky.com

Table of Contents

PART III: THE PASSIONATE WORKPLACE

For my wife, Cherisse.

My love, you are the reason I have the freedom and faith to pursue a passion-centered life. If not for your belief in me, surely my passion would have remained undiscovered.

Acknowledgements

Like the Sherpas of Mt. Everest, there are many who carried my load when it became too heavy for me to reach my summit. For each of these amazing people, I want to express my heartfelt gratitude. If not for their friendship, support and honesty, *The Passion-Centered Person* would be nothing more than a distant dream.

To my wonderful wife and best friend, Cherisse, who helped me discover my passion during a midnight conversation that set the course for the rest of my life. To my daughter, Nicole, my passion and princess that Daddy will always hold dear to my heart. Mark and Leigh Ann, you have brought to your dad the power of forgiveness. To my dear friend and co-writer Tim Vandehey, who has taken my deepest thoughts and put them to paper. And Rickey, thanks for putting up with the craziness of my life and making it all work.

A special thanks to Duane Cheney, Dr. Mark Douglas, Milton Broussard, Chet Carson, Brett Allen, Dr. Tyler Pendergrass, Dr. John York, Rick Sanchez, Jason Harper, Rick Cole, Rickey Sanchez, Scott Hagan, Adam Armstrong, The Bro's at BOB, Jeff Evans, Rod Jones, and Randy Santee.

Joe Zelesky, though you have passed away, your passion for life is revealed in the way I now live mine. I love and miss you.

Foreword

Few things in business are discussed more and understood less than passion. Passion is all the rage, a genuine buzzword. Passion is reflected in statements such as, "I am giving 110%." People respect passion. Employers desire passion in their employees. Customers are drawn to passion in a salesperson. Passion has undeniable market value, yet it is misunderstood.

To understand what passion is, it is first important to understand what it is not. Passion is often confused with emotion. People who are excitable, positive and loud are often seen as passionate. But passion has nothing to do with emotion. Passion is in fact a choice. People of passion are passionate because they choose to be. My wife Valerie and I have been married for 25 years. The reason is that I decided a long time ago not to allow the way I feel to dictate my passion. I am passionate about my wife because I choose to be passionate about her.

Let's be honest: feelings come and go. Emotions are liars even on their best day. They change with the wind. Emotions can shift from one thing to the next six times as you look over a lunch menu. Emotions swing from one extreme to another. Why make emotions your gauge of your passion? Passion, if it is to serve you, can never be based on something as unpredictable as your emotions. Passion occurs whenever you make the right decisions, regardless of how you feel. If you do the right thing, the right feeling will follow.

So what is passion? Passion is the element that makes a difference in individual lives, corporations and families. Passion is what sets great people apart from average ones and excellent companies apart from average ones. Passion is a key ingredient if you are to lead or live with any amount of effectiveness.

Passion, like many things, has defining characteristics. Asking "What is passion?" is like asking "What does milk taste like?" The answer is different for everyone, but there are some consistent qualities. My list of those qualities is not exhaustive, but it does show the building blocks for creating passion in your life.

CONVICTION—Conviction is not mental or physical—it is something that you *feel*. Something is at work. Something is encouraging you, challenging you, and guiding you. Your convictions are shaping you.

CONFIDENCE—Confidence means that you believe. The business world's quota for liars is full. People are trying to convince us of things they themselves do not believe. Confidence is inseparable from passion. You can only be passionate about things you are confident in. Such confidence is only possible with something that has captured your beliefs.

COURAGE—Courage means that you are willing to do what it takes—to risk. Businesses do not lack passion due to a lack of opportunity or market share. Businesses and individuals fail due to a lack of guts. Too many leaders today lack courage, and courage comes from passion. There is a difference between a big thinker and a big doer.

CREDIBILITY—Credibility is something you can't fake. Credibility is the passion factor that allows people to believe in you. There is an element of trust and belief in leadership. Your subordinates are always asking themselves, "Are you worth following?" There is a difference between a person struggling to lead himself and a person capable of leading others. Many people in business have the first three items on this list, but they lack credibility. For that reason they lack results.

CHARACTER—If you have character, you are transformed by your passion. True passion will consume you, and as it does it changes your actions, thoughts, words and even the way you see people. Leaders who are not consumed by what they believe, yet suggest others be consumed by it, worry me. If your passion is not changing you, give up the thought of its changing somebody else.

COMMUNICATION—Communication is sharing your passion. Passion directs your conversations. When you are passionate, your passion becomes what you always want to talk about. When you are passionate, your communication will reflect that passion. Think about what you spend the most time discussing; chances are that is your passion.

CONTAGION—Passion, like everything in leadership, is contagious. Passion is a tool that effective leaders know how to use. Passion can rally support. Passion creates credibility and ignites excitement in others. That is the power of leadership. It sets the track that others run on. Unfortunately for many leaders, they are not leading with passion. They lead with fear, guilt or insecurity. Those characteristics are also contagious. Many leaders expect their followers to achieve a level of passion that they themselves do not have. How can I expect my employees to be more passionate about my product than I am? How can I model negativity and fear and expect my employees to come to work with confidence? If customers are not excited about your product, maybe it's because everyone they encounter who represents the product lacks passion.

—Brett Allen, author, speaker and leadership trainer

Preface

No book is produced alone, and here I thank my friends and brothers who have helped me to make this book a reality by letting me share their stories of passion. Gentlemen, you honor yourselves and me. The greatest endorsements are from those who truly know you!

—Z.

When I met Gary we immediately hit it off. He was the new kid on the block; he didn't know I was a dentist and I didn't know he was involved in speaking. He got me involved in doing some team building in my office, and some life coaching. He truly enriched my life.

The most primal thing I feel about Gary's passion message is him—his enthusiasm for life, a zest that I and a lot of my colleagues have lost for one reason or another. Many of us have found that we've lost our love for our practice and our professional associations. Gary's life is all about rekindling or finding that passion. It's a cathartic experience, what I've been involved in.

My work with Gary has opened my eyes to things I had not been giving enough credence to in my life. He says, "I'm not a psychologist," but he uses similar tools to bring things to the surface. He calls you on the lies you're telling yourself. I think we develop these mental constructs about what we think we should be doing or how we should be reacting. Those aren't conducive to living a passion-centered life. Gary has helped me admit to my constructs;

I've had some sessions where I ended up pretty emotional. When you're honest and truthful, it's not always comfortable.

I hope the reader will be moved by this book to discover a passion-centered life. Gary's whole mission is helping people live life to the fullest. He's had a lot of lumps and bumps in his life, but he's never lost his zeal. We've done some pretty crazy recreational things together; it's just amazing getting to know this wild and crazy man. He doesn't realize that he's in his fifties; he thinks he's a teenager. He should be starting to simmer down in life and he's not. I hope he never does.

—*Mark Douglas, DDS*

~

You don't have to be with Gary Zelesky for more than a minute to see that he has an incredible fire for life, people, family and friends. He radiates personality and charisma. His passion is to help others discover where their own passions lie. I believe in Gary, and I believe he has a calling in his life to help people reach their God-given potential and be truly happy.

Gary constantly challenges me to dig deeper into my inner self and pull out what only God and I know is there: my passion in life. What am I really called to be? What am I here in this life to achieve? We all have a purpose for being here other than paying taxes and taking up space. One of the great challenges in life is discovering what that purpose is. Once we discover our true calling, where our passion really is, we can start moving towards our ultimate potential. Our passions not only affect us, but they have an impact on everyone we encounter. They can be blessings to others if we know how to apply them properly.

To me, the pursuit of passion is a journey of self-discovery—to understand why we are here and what God's purpose for our lives is. What gifts and strengths has He given each one of us that, if discovered and nurtured, can have an impact on our world? That is what all of us should be seeking throughout our lives.

I have several passions in my life, but the ones that consume my thoughts, time, money and energy are hunting and thinking of ways to bless others. I don't think an hour goes by that I don't think about hunting. I have to be careful not to let this passion consume me, or it can interfere with other responsibilities. I believe that God has gifted me with abilities and strengths that help me excel as a hunter, and when you are really good at something, it tends to be what you enjoy the most.

I am also passionate about blessing other people—in tangible and intangible ways. I love to be a funnel through which blessings can flow to others. We live in a world where people are constantly being torn down brick by brick by the demands of life. It is so refreshing to be able to make someone feel good about himself or bless him with some form of help he wasn't expecting. I feel like I am making a difference in a life.

Sometimes I wish God had given me talents and strengths that would have a greater impact on this world, but a part of discovering and pursuing your passions is learning to accept and love the strengths and talents God blessed you with. We may not understand why He chose these gifts, but we know we can do much with them.

—Chet Carsten

~

Gary had started on this book before I met him. He came to my company and coached me and my team, and when he did I saw the value in what he was saying.

For me, passion is about getting up in the morning and pursuing life. When he was coaching me, he was going through a process and getting to know me. I was holding myself back from being more successful, but he unearthed the core of what would thrill me every day from a personal perspective. Gary really opened my eyes, because to think that we can actually live a life in which we're pursuing our passion is just incredible. When you don't let society influence you, that's empowering.

Gary's help made me realize that it's not what I wanted to do inside Business Advantage that was the point, it's what I wanted to do with my life, period. I had to get to a point where I was willing to give up my company, because there was a chance that might not turn out to be where I was meant to be. Fortunately, that wasn't the case, but if it had worked out that way, I would have been prepared to go where my passion led.

I recently went through chemotherapy for cancer, and now I'm cancer-free. The experience of going through that has changed my perspective on pursuing your passion. Time is short. When you add up all the minutes you have, that's what your life is. You don't want to spend it just existing. When you pursue your passion, you end up with a more fulfilled life. I didn't have an awakening after cancer, because I was already awake through the three years of work I'd done with Gary. Facing death and cancer was not traumatic, because I was already living the way I wanted to.

My only question now is, can I do what I love longer? If you're in touch with your passions and pursuing them daily, bigger issues aren't as big. When you don't live with the weight of regret, facing a crisis doesn't seem as impossible.

I hope for readers this book will be the difference between success and significance. Success is not so hard to come by. But at the end of life, you want to be able to look back and say, "I'm fulfilled, I made a difference, I counted, I was significant." I think if people read this book and pursue their passions, that's going to result in a happier life. Right now, many of them are living in a way that is counter to what they really want to be doing. But it doesn't have to be that way any longer.

One of the things Gary taught me is that we cling to roles and norms—things we've been taught that just aren't true. I had placed an artificial constraint on my business. Gary asked why, and I said I didn't think I could let it grow larger without sacrificing my family.

Gary asked in that Cheshire cat "Are you pulling my leg?" voice he has, "Who taught you that?" Nobody did; it was an assumption I had made. He told me that the people who end up with no family and marriage are the ones who don't have a coach and a plan. You can be wildly successful in your business and marriage as long as you don't live blindly. Live with vision. That's what this book teaches.

—*Duane Cheney*
President & CEO, Business Advantage Consulting

~

I was introduced to the idea of this book as a coaching client of Gary's. I had been praying for an opportunity to get involved in, and with my experiences with Gary, I did not even need to think twice. I was excited from the beginning. What hit me personally about the project was Gary himself. Just working with him got me excited; he has that effect on people.

The reason I care so much about Gary's message is that I feel that pursuing passion should be enjoyable—it should not be work. You should enjoy every minute of what you are doing. That's the feeling I had as a young adult in the health club business. I looked forward to going to work. I could not wait to get started, and once I got started it was hard to leave. I have been blessed to have many jobs that, even though they may have had their bumps in the road, I have thoroughly enjoyed.

My real passion is helping people achieve their personal goals. I'm in the fireworks business now, which doesn't seem to have anything in common with my passion, but look deeper. When I sell fireworks, I don't really sell fireworks. I provide nonprofits—church groups, youth groups—with the opportunity to make money for their organizations by selling fireworks. Selling fireworks is the vehicle that serves my passion.

What I hope readers will take from this book is a clearer understanding of what their one true passion is. What is the one thing that is so important to them that when they are doing it, the first feeling when they wake up in the morning is excitement? Everyone has a passion, and I feel blessed at being part of something that is helping others discover it.

—*Milton Broussard*

~

When I first saw Gary speak in California, a lot of his stories related to me. I believed in what he was saying so much that I brought him in to speak to our district meeting of dentists. His ideas made me want to go forward with my passion, and I knew this book would do the same for people.

The driving force behind my involvement is Gary's message and knowing that it will change people's lives. By reading stories about other people's lives, we often find inspiration that helps us change our own lives by being who we were always meant to be.

My passions are working hard and playing hard. I love being a dentist. I have never regretted coming to work a day in my life. My career is really my passion, but I also take a lot of pleasure in bringing out the passions of the people I work with. One of my staff members came to me and said, "You're not going to like hearing this, but I now have a passion for going back to school." She wanted to pursue a nursing career. Gary gave me and my staff that drive to know we're not too old; we can move forward and find the things that motivate us. In dentistry, I see a life change in every patient I touch, and that's wonderful. I hope readers will see the same thing and make that positive spirit inside them come out.

We're all passionate about our own things, from the sports we play to the jobs we do and the way we live. If someone finds that within himself, he will have a more fulfilling life. It's part of Maslow's triangle of the inner self: following your passion is about finding self-actualization. It's about not letting anyone tell you that you can't do something. You just do it.

—*Ty Pendergrass, DDS*

~

Fundamentally, I believe in pouring into people: investing time, effort and resources in those who want to learn, change, meet their potential and be productive citizens. After meeting Gary, I determined that he has similar goals: helping others to identify and pursue what they truly enjoy.

Being involved in this book has encouraged me to reflect upon my past to look for the moments when I really enjoyed what I was doing. Through the exercises, I have been able to identify what I am passionate about, and then ask myself, "Why I am trying so hard to achieve success in areas that could never return the same level of satisfaction?" I discovered my need to focus my efforts on the things that will be most rewarding if I achieve them.

In my life, the pursuit of passion has been a cycle of pouring into others and myself. During the cycle I invest in the development and growth of me, my family and many people whose paths I have crossed. I have used my available resources so that each person could begin to achieve some short-term goals, get a vision, and perhaps glimpse his or her individual potential.

Now that my children are young adults, I find that I am once again realigning my resources to prepare myself for a final career choice—one that will be more in line with something I enjoy versus something that just brings home a paycheck.

I am positioning myself to realize a lifelong goal of being self-employed and seeking activities that will allow me to spend and enjoy more time with the love of my life, my wife. God willing, the cycle will go through a few more revolutions as we are blessed with our children's weddings, grandchildren, and our senior years.

My outlook has changed completely since being exposed to this material. Before, I was doing what I needed to do to make ends meet. Now, I am pursuing only what I truly want to achieve. No longer am I willing to settle for whatever comes my way. I have always said that I would not be controlled by money. In keeping with that belief, I am working on ending a lucrative career to pursue the things I am most passionate about: family and happiness. My wife and I have been apart from our families for twenty-five years, and like the prodigal son, it is time we get back home. I am trusting that my work experience, academic accomplishments and God-given talents will line me up for an opportunity to find employment and allow me to support the growth and development of those around me.

—*Rick Sanchez*

~

I chose to become involved in this project because I believe in the philosophy of the book and its author. I have seen how being a passion-centered individual has had an incredibly positive impact on not just Gary's life, but the lives of those around him as well.

The message of *The Passion-Centered Person* has been lifechanging. I look at things differently and see what I am doing through a completely different filter. I no longer look at things as though I have to put in my time to achieve what I really want. Instead I look at what I really want, and that determines what I do with my time. I have the privilege of working with Gary on a daily basis, and I have seen how he has used the filter of his passion to determine what he should be involved in. I've witnessed how that has helped him arrive at where he is today. I have also had my father as an incredible example of what discovering one's passion looks like and how following it will take you to places you never dreamed possible.

I am incredibly hopeful when it comes to the pursuit of passion in my life. I am still a college student, so I consider my ability to understand passion to be a blessing. I still have my entire life ahead of me. My passion brought me to Gary, but it will be my passion that takes me beyond Gary. I am extremely excited about what lies ahead. I feel like I have a head start in not just discovering my passion, but making it what I do.

Thanks to what I've learned from Gary, I have changed what I do with my time and where I am headed in life. I stopped working at a safe, successful job to partner with him in helping others achieve what they thought they could only imagine. I have also decided that music is a passion. I started taking drum lessons, and though I may never become Stewart Copeland of the Police, my sheer passion for music and playing the drums is more than enough for me. I also have focused my schooling down to a specific emphasis and am more focused and motivated than ever. I know my schooling is going to enable me to accomplish more than I ever thought. It will only add to my passion.

—*Rickey Sanchez*

~

In beginning this writing, it has occurred to me for the first time that my relationship with Gary, which has turned into one of my most treasured friendships, really began with *my* passion—the passion to provide the youth of my town and community an opportunity for a more promising future. Strange that the word "passion" never crossed my mind when I thought back on my first contact with Gary, but it's not surprising that something as powerful as passion can redirect the course of one's life, as it did in this instance.

There I was, in a room of 1700-plus dentists in November 1999 in Las Vegas, attending my first large-scale dental seminar. The man who stole the show that day, not only for me but all others, was not a dentist, but Gary Zelesky. I can watch the video of his presentation and relive the emotion that compelled me to pick up the phone the following Monday morning and call him. My first thought when I got on the plane to return home was "If only the kids back home could experience Gary's message. I know it would make a difference in their lives." That was the moment that I began a self-discovery process that changed the rest of my life.

My passion to make a difference overcame my apprehension

about doing something out of my comfort zone. My decision to bring Gary to our community gave the people in it the chance to be better. What he shared with others here has been unbelievable; the difference I feel he has made is immeasurable. But I wonder what would have happened if I had decided not to make that phone call? It was uncharacteristic of me. My friendship with Gary, my brother, would never have happened. What if I had not listened to my passion when it screamed at me? Where would I be today? That call changed my life. I've never been the same. I believe that my passion was always there, waiting to be released, but it took someone who displayed that same passion for others to help me accept my own passion as something I should follow. I knew the emotion I felt that day had to be shared—KNEW it would change everything.

The confidence I discovered after stepping out of my own shadow has changed the way I look at everything. The way I practice dentistry today is so much different than it was a few years ago as I continue to follow where my passion leads me. So many relationships that I have today would never have been initiated if I had not taken that first leap of faith in 1999. I've come to see that following your own passion is one of the most important things you can do for yourself—maybe *the* most important.

Releasing yourself to follow your passion is not a one-time decision, but it's not a one-time reward, either. Continue to follow your passion constantly, and the rewards are perpetual. Stretch yourself more than you allow others to stretch you. Do this and you will follow your own passion to a place where others may be able to discover their own.

This is why I am involved in Gary's book. I know what he did for me. I know what it can do for others. I know its importance because I didn't truly start living until one November day in 1999. That's a day I will never forget.

—*John York*

Introduction

How Passion Became My Passion

One of my favorite sayings is, "It's not where you start but where you finish that matters." I'm a living example of this.

When I was two years old, my parents got divorced. They not only walked out on each other, they also quite literally walked out on me. From age three to six I lived with my Aunt Aggie, a beast of a woman resembling Jabba the Hut with facial hair. My aunt had a habit of mixing her anger with alcohol, a dangerous combination that brought yelling, and often her hand across my face. Too many times, I heard from her how stupid, dumb and ignorant I was. At a time when most children need answers and reassurance, she'd explain to me that my parents got divorced because I was born. I was never meant to be here. I was the worst thing that ever happened to the Zelesky family. Needless to say, I was not raised to be a motivational speaker. Then again, I was. The sting of those words left a mark on my life and my soul for many years.

When my mother remarried, she gained full custody of my sister and me. Now, I know there are wonderful stepparents who make their love seamless between their children and their stepchildren. My stepfather was not one of them. Lou (I would never, ever call him Father) made my aunt's drinking look like amateur hour. He was a full-blown alcoholic. I became very familiar with the feeling of waking up to a belt across my back. I was no stranger to the smell of stale beer and cigarette smoke. I was on speaking terms with abuse and neglect.

Mr. Becker

Because Lou's alcoholism made it impossible for him to hold down a job, we moved a lot. I was shuffled from school to school during my grade school years. So I never made friends my own age, and was never able to find that sense of stability and safety that adolescents need. I learned never to trust anyone. Worse, I never learned to hope for anything better than what I had. I felt like I didn't *deserve* anything better. I was determined that no matter what I did, I would be met with failure and disappointment, and this bred in me a terrible attitude.

I dragged a luggage cart of emotional baggage from school to school. Childhood trauma? Throw it on the cart. Abuse? Go ahead, there's room. My cart was stacked so high that FedEx probably wouldn't touch it. This suitcase was the belt my stepfather used. This one was filled with my aunt's stinging words. I wore a defiant, negative, destructive attitude around myself like a wall of barbed wire.

When I walked into my English class as a freshman in high school, I was determined this would be the first of many sullen failures. Then Mr. Becker stopped me short. He was the oldest man I'd ever seen. He looked like he'd been born with chalk in one hand and a thick ruler in the other. Eventually I walked up to him and announced arrogantly, "I've got three goals."

He stopped to listen.

"Number one, I'm dropping out of school in three weeks. Number two, I'm taking as many students as I can with me." No reaction. "And number three, I am going to be your personal nightmare every single day until I leave."

He should have thrown me out of his class. Nobody got paid enough money to deal with a sullen, rage-filled, defiant kid like me. I was the kid you gave up on, the one you threw into some "special" program in educational Siberia to get him out of sight of the "good" kids.

But Mr. Becker just looked at me and, in a deep voice that seemed to emerge from the Abyss, said, "Welcome to my class. Go take a seat."

So I sat in his class for three weeks. He always wore the same blue jacket and talked loudly, as if we, not he, were deaf. He spit a lot; we called the front seats the Splash Zone. And after three weeks had passed, I approached him and said as matter-of-factly as I could, "Today, Gary Zelesky is dropping out of school."

I expected to see him sigh with relief. After all, I had insulted him, disrupted class, and even invited him to go with us on a class project to look for his personality. Perhaps he'd salute me, snap "Cadet, disMISSED!" and go back to his lesson plans.

But instead, Mr. Becker looked at me and said, "Son, before you go, I want you to know something. You've got po-tential!"

I shook my head. "I'm leaving, Mr. Becker."

"Z, before you go, do me a favor. Stand over by that door."

"Mr. Becker, I'm in a hurry."

"I understand. F students have heavy agendas." Ouch, I had to give him credit for that one. Harrumphing, I went to stand by the door. I would humor the old codger. I'd never have to see him again.

He went into his desk and came out with an enormously long rubber band. He cornered me against the wall and dangled the rubber band in front of my face. With a bizarre, cackling laugh that could have come from the Wicked Witch of the West, he started wiggling the rubber band so it danced before my eyes. "This is you," he said. "You move, but you're never... going... anywhere." The rubber band continued to shimmy. "Z, you are constantly in motion but you have no direction." Pause. "With your personality, I can see that in the future, you are either going to affect thousands of people, or *defect* thousands of people. Which will be up to you."

I snorted, my awful attitude welling up inside. He was having none of it. He pointed his bony finger at me and said, "Teachers point the way to the future. I don't care about where you've been. I only care about where you're going. You have to let go of your past if you are going to grab your future."

Before I could come up with a snotty retort, he suddenly pulled back on the rubber band and aimed it right at my forehead. "You will never be launched until you are stretched! Let me ask you a question: How do you like school?"

"I hate it."

The band stretched back further. "How do you like the homework I give you?"

"I hate homework." The band stretched further.

Then I saw Mr. Becker's face change and take on a look I hadn't ever expected to see from him: compassion. "What was it like to feel abandoned when you were little? What was it like being told how stupid you are, that you'll never amount to anything?"

Every time he asked a question about my painful past, he would pull the rubber band back. I was being stretched that day. But the more a rubber band is stretched, the farther it will fly when it's let go. Pain becomes gain, though I couldn't see that at the time.

"What was it like when your stepfather hit you? Where did you put all that hurt?"

Tears were rolling down my face. "Mr. Becker, I hate you."

"No you don't," he said calmly. "You hate all the people who never took the time to believe in you. But most of all, you hate yourself." He pulled the rubber band back to arm's length. It was now stretched tight as a wire and still aimed at the center of my forehead. Mr. Becker's face was grim as his fingers twitched. "Z, when you graduate high school, you will be the rubber band." With a surprising yelp he let the rubber band go. I closed my eyes, anticipating a wicked sting, but I heard it pass my right ear. It flew out the door and smacked another kid on his way to class square in the head.

"Mr. Becker, that was an incredible shot!"

"Today is not about rubber bands, Z. Today is about grabbing hold of your future."

I stayed in school. This wasn't a fairy tale; things didn't change for me overnight. I still wallowed in the memories of hurt. What we don't realize is that the people who hurt us in the past are *still* hurting us when they are keeping us from moving toward our future. Long after I was too big for my stepfather to hit, I still cringed at the pains in my memory. Long after Aunt Aggie had died, I let her words burn me. But Mr. Becker's lesson had not been lost on me. I began to understand that we have to let the past be our teacher and not our reality. We have to let it instruct us and otherwise let it go. Instead, we must let the future be our challenge. Your future is your challenge, and it begins now.

My Passion for Passion

Perhaps to compensate for all I went through as a child, I've developed a very outgoing personality. I love speaking to people and speaking with them—not at them. When I speak at an event, I'm as thrilled being with my audience one-on-one after I speak as I am in speaking to them from the podium. And I love stories. People love to tell me their stories, and I love to listen. Many times when I was on the road years ago giving motivational speeches, audience members would come up to me after my speech and tell me their stories. This would go on for hours, but I never got tired of it.

I remember thinking, "Man, these people are really passionate about their stories." I mentioned this to my wife, Cherisse, and wished I could feel the same way. At that point I had been speaking professionally in some capacity for more than twenty years, and the fire just wasn't there. I felt like all I was doing was flying from place to place and cashing checks. There wasn't any purpose behind it. I didn't feel like I was doing what I was supposed to be doing. Most importantly, I didn't feel like my speaking was making a difference in people's lives. I needed something more.

I'm a believer in what Carl Jung called *synchronicities*, those too-fortunate-to-be-random coincidences. About that time I experienced one. We were walking through an airport and my wife spotted a book at a bookstore. It was called *The Brand Called You*, by Peter Montoya and Tim Vandehey. We bought the book, and it changed my life. This book was about how to brand your life, and the most important piece of advice I got from it was that you had to figure out the one thing that describes you. Focused on passion as I was, to me that meant, "What is your passion?" The problem was, I didn't know.

Cherisse and I read that book for weeks and talked about my passion. Nothing quite seemed to fit me. Then one night about midnight, she sat up in bed and said, "I know what your passion is." I was half asleep, so I probably just grunted and rolled over. "Your passion is passion!"

Now I was awake. This made sense. She continued. "You can sit and listen to someone talk about their passion for hours." She's right. Cherisse says I'm the kind of person who can go down to San Francisco and watch a street performer for hours, because he has such passion for what he's doing. I went to a funeral once and after it was over, I talked to the funeral director for a long time. I heard about how he takes care of the family and embalms the body and everything, and I got so excited about his passion for his work that I went back the next day and went into the back rooms to see how he did his job.

Passion was and is my passion. Nothing has ever been more clear to me.

Passion Changes Everything

I became a student of all things related to passion. I became a "passionist." I found that a person's physical posture changes when he's talking about his position at work and then suddenly shifts to talking about his passion. His shoulders go from slumped to square, and his arms go from crossed to gesturing with excitement. I've helped people feel like that every day, and I wouldn't trade it for the world.

After that discovery, I made the decision to make passion the study of my life. I had been speaking, but I wasn't fulfilled by it; I felt like I was called to bring people more than a temporary motivational fix. The more I looked for and learned about passion, the more I saw its lack. I know an incredibly successful speaker who made a million dollars last year and is still searching for her passion. The money isn't enough for her; she needs more. That just shows you that successful people can still be outside their passion.

One of the best parts of my passion journey has been my friendship with my co-author, Tim Vandehey. After Cherisse read *The Brand Called You*, she said, "I'm going to call him and ask him about helping you write your book." She did, and Tim did. Now he and I have become dear friends. That's what passion does. It produces a new position in life. In our case, it created a new relationship. Tim's and my passion for life has created our future—a future I never could have imagined from the vantage point of Mr. Becker's classroom.

My sincere hope is that this book will do the same for you. Let's see what happens. Ready to be stretched?

Gary Zelesky
Sacramento, California
August 2007

Part I:

The Elements of Passion

Chapter One

The Riches of a Passionate Life

What is passion? It is surely the becoming of a person. Are we not, for most of our lives, marking time? Most of our being is at rest, un-lived. In passion, the body and the spirit seek expression outside of self. Passion is all that is other from self. Sex is only interesting when it releases passion. The more extreme and the more expressed that passion is, the more unbearable does life seem without it. It reminds us that if passion dies or is denied, we are partly dead and that soon, come what may, we will be wholly so.

—John Boorman, British filmmaker

"Gary, I hate my life."

I was speechless, and I'm a professional speaker. The gentleman in front of me was the epitome of the prosperous professional—a successful dentist with a thriving practice, an expensive suit, and probably a high-performance German car in his garage. Yet as he spoke his voice was hushed and broken with suppressed emotion, as if he were close to tears. It was like he was confessing his most terrible secret.

"I make all this money, and I hate what I do," he continued. I asked him about his work and his life, but what I wanted to know was very simple: Did he know what his passion was? Was he expressing that passion in his work? Or was he doing what so many

professionals do: burying his passion, ignoring the agony of abandoned dreams and numbing the pain with expensive toys? Looking
at this man who by any conventional measure was wildly successful, I already knew the answers.

This is not an unusual situation for me. In my work as a speaker
and personal coach, I have encountered hundreds of wealthy professionals—physicians, lawyers, dentists, stockbrokers, entrepreneurs—who, despite the fact that they make a ton of money, enjoy
the respect of their peers and spend their days making stimulating,
challenging decisions, despise what they do. They dread the beginning of the workday, live for all-too-brief vacations, and look forward to retirement the way a man on mile 15 of a marathon looks forward to a foot massage. The money? It's great, but the more of it they
accumulate, the more meaningless it becomes. And all along, there's
a terrible aching void inside them they can't explain and can't fill.
Ironically, they can't even complain about their misery. After all,
who's going to listen to a millionaire whine and moan about his or
her life?

Passion is the Difference

When you look in the mirror each morning, do you see those
emotions in your own face? You don't have to be a tycoon to experience them; there's no income test for feeling lost in the career
you've built. It can happen to anyone, from a CEO to the owner of
a one-person business.

Now look at a different kind of professional, one who works
long days without ever seeming to become tired and fills the room
with energy and life. He attracts great people to his cause without
trying, and even though he doesn't worry about money, he never
seems to lack it. He's a boundless source of creative ideas, a leader
who inspires everyone else to exceed their limitations. He approaches
even his failures with optimism and confidence in his eventual victory.

What's the difference between the two? *Passion*. The second
person has discovered and embraced his passion and made it the

center of his working life. He still has to pay bills, deal with people he doesn't like and take out the garbage, just like the rest of us, but because he spends each day doing something that makes him feel lucky to be alive, he's vibrant, magnetic and unstoppable.

Which kind of professional are you? A few questions:

- Do I look forward to each workday or dread it?

- Do I spend any part of my day doing what I love?

- Does my time working fly by or crawl by?

- Would I do my work if I didn't get paid or quit if that didn't mean losing my lifestyle?

- Do I envy those who do what they love, regardless of what they earn, or do I feel lucky to do what I do?

- If I could live my life over again, would I still do what I do?

Passion is the Power to Transform Your Career

If you're excited just to get up every morning, you're blessed. If not, you have a lot of company: an October 2005 survey by Korn/Ferry International of 2,160 senior executives worldwide found that 51 percent said that if they could start their careers over again, they would do something completely different—pursue their dreams of being everything from astronauts to professional athletes. They would build their careers around their passions.

Passion is what I'm here to talk to you about. Passion is the missing ingredient in a million careers, the force that launches a thousand new businesses, turns people with daring visions into the heralds of new industries, and makes routine tasks cause for joy. Meteorologists claim that a hurricane is the most powerful heat engine and energy generator on earth; I disagree. Passion is a hurricane of life force, with the power to transform your career into a labor of love or to blow you toward a new business, a new path, or an unexplored talent you barely remember you possess.

We live in a world where too many of us lock our passion away in a dim room when we leave college and spend the next 50 years pretending we don't hear it pounding on the door. I'm going to show you how to throw that door open, tear the whole blasted building down and rebuild a passion-centered professional life that rewards you in more ways than you could ever imagine.

I speak before thousands of professionals every year, and I talk to hundreds of them personally. As I said, I love hearing personal stories. But many of the people in my audiences are telling me what they don't like about what they do, and that's educational. It's given me a window into the mindset of the busy, highly-educated professional that most people don't have. You see, I think it's tempting these days to look at someone with a huge house, a swimming pool and a BMW as someone who must therefore be happy. But that's not the case. It's a cliché, but money really does not buy happiness.

What are the most common reasons I hear that otherwise "successful" professionals are miserable in their work? It comes down to five major ones:

- They don't feel appreciated by anyone, often including their families.

- They feel trapped by obligations and have a secret thing they would love to be doing, but worry about not being able to make a living at it.

- They're just plain bored.

- They feel like what they do compromises their values in some way.

- They feel their talents are not being used or recognized.

Any of those sound familiar? Why are you feeling unhappy or lost in what you do? Don't despair; your passion is here to change things forever.

What is Passion?

The kind of passion I'm talking about has nothing to do with sex. Your passion is that single thing you were born to do or to be. It's the life occupation that you would spend your day doing even if you were never paid a dime, the pursuit that can keep you up all night working, never feeling fatigued, only to be surprised by the sunrise into saying, "Wow. What time is it?" Your passion isn't to be confused with your *passions*, which are those things that you enjoy doing, like woodcarving or playing the guitar. Your passion is your highest, best purpose. It's your calling.

Passion builds, creates, invents, takes risks, renews, changes thought, and transforms nations. It maximizes the mundane and minimizes misfortune. It's the creative fire of a million Picassos or Gaudis, a force that fuels innovation and defies the impossible. It's the raw material of a thousand childhood dreams. Jane Goodall followed it to Africa, Jacques Cousteau followed it to the deepest oceans, and Benjamin Franklin used it to light the world and found a new nation. Passion can't be faked; it speaks more truth about who you are and what you stand for than all the marketing plans in the world. Passion moves hearts and compels people to do extraordinary deeds for others. Living in pure passion is as close as we come to fulfilling our God-given calling.

Don't mistake passion for obsession. While passion can occupy the center of your life, obsession drives your life. While passion is about serving others, obsession is a compulsion that knows only its own need. While passion creates, obsession can stunt or destroy. Witness the obsession with money that brought down corporations from Enron to WorldCom, and you see what I mean.

In my speaking engagements, I often find that people equate living big—big car, big house, big personality—with living passionately. Not so. Passion is a river. It's not about the width of the water, but its depth. Professionals who are living and working with passion are continually trying new ways to express that passion—testing, examining, proving, inspecting, appraising and judging new pursuits. But in the end, they're always making their channel narrower and deeper. They are honing in on a single purpose while maintaining a broad vision for their lives. Lives that make a difference to one other person or the world are narrow and deep, not shallow and wide. Remember, big doesn't always mean deep. To mix my metaphors, the passion-centered professional focuses the spotlight of his passion until it becomes a high-intensity laser.

The Million-Dollar Question

So why am I coming to you, dear reader, with all this talk about passion? Isn't passion for lovers or starving artists? NO! Passion makes the difference between leading a life you love and a life you merely tolerate. Let me make my point by citing the first of my Passion Principles:

> *If your passion isn't part of what you do,*
> *you will never be rich.*

Sure, you might make money. You might live in a huge house and have a TV larger than my car. But you will never lead a rich life filled with purpose. You will never know the delight of spending your time doing something that feeds your soul instead of your bank account.

If you're tempted to dismiss this as touchy-feely, ask yourself this: How many of your peers have burned out? How many men and women you know who were earning fortunes and building empires gave it all up because they couldn't take the stress, the Faustian bargains, the emptiness? You're not a money making machine. You're a human being, hard-wired to dream and explore. If you deny that side of your nature 50 hours a week for 40 years, you won't be able to sustain the effort it takes to create any kind of success. You may be feeling that way already.

Before you worry that I'm going to spend the next 200 pages

trying to convince you to move to Alaska and become a mountain man, or trash your law practice to live in an old-growth redwood (I'm not), let me ask you something vital:

What could you achieve if the only question you had to ask to know if something was right for your career was, "Am I passionate about it?"

No worrying about if it makes you money. No caring about what your peers think. Just *does it serve your passion?* What could you accomplish if your passion, the thing that gives you the most pure joy, was your only criterion for making career decisions? How much more energy would you bring to each day? What would you create? How many people would you inspire? How rich would you become if your mission was to share your passion with as many people as possible and let it come to life in them?

It is possible. We are meant to live passionately every day, not just when we have the time. Instead of being exhausted by thoughts of the next day, you have the birthright to be exuberant in the here and now. People do it every day, people with at least as much trepidation and doubt as you have. You can do it, too. It takes courage and commitment and vision and strength, but you already have those qualities. All you need to do is find your passion. The good news is, it never went away.

What We'll Achieve in This Book

If you've made it this far, you're feeling that ache. I know it well. Before I discovered my calling, I wondered if boarding planes and cashing checks was all there was to life. If that's the stage you're at in your profession, you're at the right place at the right time. *The Passion-Centered Professional* is about helping professionals in all fields rediscover the passion that's inside them, no matter how deeply it's buried, developing that passion, then applying that passion in their work.

For some people reading this book, that will mean re-focusing their current business, maybe working in a more narrow field that they find fascinating. For others, the change will be more radical. They will decide to chuck it all and devote themselves to the thing they loved to do before they got stuck on the treadmill—music, painting, politics, who knows? Still others will take the thing they love to do today and turn it into a business. Passion is at the heart of every entrepreneur. Which will you do? We'll make that discovery together as we go.

If you still have your doubts that passion will lead to greater professional success, let me share something else with you. In my work helping thousands of professionals to revitalize their passions and put them to work in their careers, I've discovered a wonderful cyclical path that all people who embrace their passion end up walking. It goes like this:

1. **Passion**—You find a way to make what you love part of your work every day. It could be starting a completely new career or simply weaving your calling into the work you're doing now.

2. **Productivity**—Powered by the joy and energy that comes with

releasing your passion, you get more done. You innovate, take risks, work harder, and arouse the passions of others to do the same.

3. Profit—As a result of your greater productivity, you earn more financial profit AND more spiritual, emotional profit. Your company grows. Your relationships improve. New opportunities appear. People sense the authentic passion in what you create and buy it. It's better than any advertising.

4. Pleasure—You have more money to do the things you love to do. You have greater fulfillment every day. You feel a sense of purpose and pride. Life is no longer just about earning a paycheck, but about creating and reaching out.

The great thing is that once you reach #4, you cycle back to Passion and start again! Pleasure makes you even more enthusiastic about pursuing your passion, so the cycle continues. This kind of "cycle of energy" turns your passion into the engine for your professional success.

Whatever you have achieved in your career so far, there's more you want to do, or you wouldn't be reading this book. Maybe you've made your money but want to make a difference. Or you haven't achieved financial freedom, but crave it. Or you just wonder, "Is this all there is?" In the race to build your career, your company, your practice or your resume, you left your passion in the rear view mirror because it wasn't practical, didn't appear profitable, or was simply terrifying. Now it's time to reclaim it.

The Day I Got a Painting in the Mail

Pound-for-pound, kids have more passion than 95 percent of the adults on this planet. Sometimes it seems like kids *are* pure passion given form by scuffed sneakers, baseball caps and patched jeans. As children, we all start with passion. We love everything we see, the novelty and wonder of it. We want to be firefighters, scientists, rock stars, teachers, mountain climbers. When we're children, our passions are like flower bulbs just waiting for sun and water to sprout and grow. But all too often, children are told to "stop being such dreamers," and to grow up and be practical. Parents wield incredible power over their children's passions, and if they bury those passions early, they can stay buried for decades.

On one speaking engagement, I met a dentist in his 60s who told me that when he was a child, he loved to paint more than anything else. But when he showed his mother his work, his mother discouraged him, saying, "You're not the artist in the family." That sounds awful now, but the mother wasn't being cruel, just thoughtless. Little did she know those few words would lead her son to give up any thoughts of being an artist for many, many years.

The story, however, has a happy ending. This man told me that because of what I had said in my speech, he was going to dig up his passion for painting and give it another try. I was delighted to hear it, but then I went off to more speeches and more work and forgot about him. Then, about three months later, I got a package in the mail. It was a painting from the man, along with a note thanking me for re-awakening him to something that had brought him such pure joy. He had been painting ever since that day and had brought positive change to his life.

Passion Never Dies, It Just Gets Buried

That story is proof of something that I try to make sure every single person I speak to understands: passion cannot be killed, only buried. Like the flower bulb, when passion is attacked or hurt, it goes dormant. Eventually, we cover our passion with more layers of obligation: school, work, family, debt and so on. And there our passion sits, waiting.

We never forget about that quiescent passion; every now and then it will sting us, as if to remind us what we've turned our backs on. A man who loved playing the saxophone as a teenager will walk by a jazz club, hear the wail of an alto sax and feel a momentary stab of loss. A woman who dreamed of backpacking around the globe but never left her hometown might channel surf past a travel program and feel a hole open in the pit of her stomach where all her adventures should have been. When it comes to our buried passions, we make a bargain with ourselves: we'll pretend not to feel the sting of regret, and our passion will not whisper to us, asking us to upset a life that, while not joyous, is at least predictable and safe.

That, my friends, is no way to live! When you start exploring your passion, you start digging. You throw up shovelfuls of earth until you find what you thought you had lost, but you don't remove the dirt. Instead, you turn it into a rich soil of forgiveness, faith and energy. You use the experiences of your past to fuel the passion of your present. And what do you find? That passion you buried all those years ago has been waiting for you, just waiting for you to pick it up again.

The Four Layers of Buried Passion

You have a right to know what you are called to do and to live out your passion in your career. But the discovery of one's passion is not reserved for "the right moment." There's no right time to find that thing that fills you with endless energy, no such thing as "I can't afford to find my passion right now." Passion doesn't wait until you have all your ducks in a row to turn your life upside down. It just does. As soon as you start digging, it's only a matter of time before you have this new, uncontrollable force in your life.

But what's in the soil you're digging through? It's important to know this, because as you begin to look deep within to find your passion, you're going to stumble upon obstacles that are as hard to move as rocks and as tough as tree roots. These are the factors that buried your passion in the first place and kept you from trying to find it for all these years. Only if you recognize them for what they are can you dig around them and get to the heart of the matter.

There are four layers of buried passion:

1. Pain. Pain is trying to tell you something is wrong, but it can also make you stronger. I had an abusive stepfather, but his abuses only made me stronger in the pursuit of my passion, which is to communicate with others about passion. Pain makes you recoil and drop your passion like it's hot, and it becomes easier to let it sit on the ground than to pick it up and risk the pain again. But to find your passion, you must forgive and embrace the pain. It only hurts if you let it.

2. **Anger:** Anger is misplaced passion. You can turn your anger inward and rage at yourself for letting your passion go for so long, but what purpose does that serve? Or you can send anger outward to destroy the things in the way of your passion, but will that change the past? There's only one thing to do with anger: channel it. Use your anger to fuel your passion, to motivate you to recapture your passion and make changes in your life and the lives of others.

3. **Fear:** The opposite of passion is not apathy, but fear. However, there are two kinds of fear: the fear that comes when you're about to step off a cliff into the unknown, and the fear that prevents you from getting to the edge of the cliff at all. One is thrilling; the other is paralyzing. If you are in your passion, you will never feel more truly alive than when you are afraid—afraid of uncertainty, failure and risk. Fear is passion's way of telling you, "Yes, you're on the right road." If you're not afraid, you're not living in your passion. The paralyzing fear is ancient history. It's the fear that made you believe you couldn't make a living following your passion, that you weren't good enough. That fear should be buried in the hole that used to hold your passion. Good riddance.

4. **Love:** Wait, I thought love is all you need! That's what the Beatles said! Love is the heart of passion, but it can also be misused. If love turns into a lust for those things that are just about gratifying your short-term desires, then you've got obsession. Instead, love should be about creating and giving to others, not to mention finding the love of your life. Remember, passion is selfless; it's about creating opportunities for others to thrive, not just yourself. If you can grow to apply your passion to the world, not just yourself, you're ready to make a career out of what you love.

A Life Without Regret

Speaker and author Jim Rohn said, "We must all suffer from one of two pains: the pain of discipline or the pain of regret. The difference is that discipline weighs ounces while regret weighs tons." Have you ever wondered what it is that makes your days at the office seem so oppressive, or makes you feel like Sisyphus endlessly pushing his boulder uphill in Hell when you drive to work? It's regret. Regret is an invisible jacket that drapes around your shoulders, and each year, as you deny your passion out of fear, laziness or simple inertia, it grows a little heavier. Because the increase in weight is gradual, you barely notice. But after 20 years doing something you hate, you're weighed down, bent practically double by the paths of life that you didn't explore. Regret weighs tons? Darned right.

But what happens when you say "Enough" and remove the coat? You feel reborn. The weight is gone. You feel more than a spring in your step; you feel like you can jump over buildings. That's how people who work in their passion feel every day. They are doing something they adore, something they're good at, something that makes them feel they've really accomplished something at the end of the day. I think I feel a Passion Principle coming on:

> *To build a career around passion*
> *is to live without regret.*

Why do we regret? We rarely regret the actions we take (the exception might be in our romantic relationships). We regret the things we DON'T do—the opportunities we miss, the ships that sail. But if you have built your professional life firmly around your passion, you won't miss those opportunities. When the chance to start a business or relocate to a foreign country comes along, you'll ask that question: "Does this speak to my passion?" If it does, you'll be off and running! The only opportunities you'll miss are the ones that don't matter.

I want to spare you the pain of undiscovered, unfulfilled passion. Left in the ground, passion does more than slumber: it rusts. It corrodes, and eventually that corrosion spreads to your heart. You become hard and angry and resentful of people who have followed their passions and built the careers and lives you should have built but did not.

If I can do nothing else in this book, I want to teach you how to live without regret. I think there's no worse phrase in the English language than, "I wish I would have…" There's so much bereavement in those words. More than that, there's hopelessness. Passion is hope. It's the hope that there is always a way to make life sweeter, more profitable and more productive tomorrow than it is today.

What's Your Perfect Day?

We're not just talking about passion in life, but in your career. We're looking at how you can become a passion-centered professional—someone who incorporates your highest, most fervent purpose into your work life in some way, so that what you do for a living actually propels you to live more ecstatically and greet each work day with anticipation and delight. To do that, you've got to decide what your perfect day at work looks like.

Try this: write down your perfect day in detail. It can be anywhere, with anyone, with one condition: it's got to be a day at work. No days on the beach in Barbuda; you must be doing something to make a living, being productive. What would that day look like? Would you do what you're doing now? Would you do something completely different? Or would you keep doing what you're doing but make wholesale changes? There is no right answer. The first step to creating your perfect work life is imagining what it would be. That's where your professional passion lies.

That's my cue for another Passion Principle, perhaps the most important one of all:

Your passion for life creates your position in life.

When you follow your passion—or more accurately, when you turn it loose to run free, dragging you behind like a Great Dane owner barely holding onto the leash—you will create opportunity. People will come into your life, attracted by your vision and excitement. Look at the great activists of our day, from Bono of U2 to Bob Geldof, creator of Live Aid. How did they get so many superstars and political leaders from all over the world to put in thousands of hours for their causes for no financial reward? It was the strength of their passion.

When you interweave your passion with your profession, you will find that you get more done. Because you care about what you're doing, you're more productive. When work is drudgery, you can't wait to think about something else—anything else. But when it's enjoyable, your mind is always active and coming up with new ideas. That's where innovation comes from. Bringing your passion into your career motivates you to do more, be more and take control of your future in ways you might never have considered. It's amazing what can happen when what you do for a living also delights and surprises you.

Entrepreneurs Sell Passion

From Steve Jobs of Apple Computer to Sean Fanning, the college kid who started Napster and turned the music world on its head, entrepreneurship is about passion above all else. Yes, there's the potential for big money and excitement. But I defy you to find one successful entrepreneur whose idea for a new business didn't keep him awake at night, until he had no choice but to look for venture capital just to get some sleep. Even the most business-savvy entrepreneur begins with passion; without it, no one would endure the risk, the endless workdays, the uncertainty and the caffeine.

Passion and the endless innovation it breeds are the soul of entrepreneurship. In fact, entrepreneurs sell passion more than products. They ask investors, new employees and customers not just to buy, but to *believe*—in their vision, their idea, their passion.

As a result, passion changes the landscape. Creative, business-savvy individuals tap the energy of passion to bring to life new technologies and ways of doing business—transforming business, commerce and society in the process. If change is not occurring, then passion is absent.

Are You Doing What You Love?

Are you done planning your perfect day at work? Good. Now, how much of that perfect day are you living right now? I frequently ask my audiences and coaching clients, "What percentage of what you love doing is used in your career?" The most common answer: Zero. That's a tragedy, but it's not surprising. Your passion will always enhance your position, but your position seldom enhances your passion.

Companies continue to hire people for the wrong reasons and then wonder why they don't function at their maximum potential. That's because they are hired to plug holes and solve problems. In most companies, employees are hardly encouraged to express their passions. Corporations worry that creative, passionate employees will get the itch to leave and start their own companies, and they're right. That's what innovative people do! Most major corporations started because someone got sick of working for someone else, of just coming in to collect a paycheck, and tapped his passion to build something new. So the question isn't why do passionate employees leave, but why can't corporations create cultures that foster and reward passion?

You can do your job, but you can only live your passion. To be fair, most of us are forced to do something we like while we're looking for a way to make a living doing what we love. There's nothing wrong with that. But it goes bad when we become so involved with what we like that we confuse it for what we love. If we're good at it, we assume that's our passion. Not necessarily. I hear people all the time who say, "I'm really good at what I do, but it's not my passion," or "I've spent my whole life doing what I am trained for, but not what I love." Or my favorite, "Hey, it's a living!" to which I respond, "Yes, but is it a life?" It's not asking too much to have *both*.

Burn Those Tickets to Alaska

Many of the people I work with on finding their passion hesitate because they think a passion-filled career means disrupting the career they have now, throwing everything they've built into the trash and starting over from scratch. Now, I told you I wasn't going to ask you to move to Alaska and become a mountain man, and I meant it. Embracing your passionate profession doesn't have to mean a complete disruption of your career. Your passion will tell you how it needs to be expressed. When you're in touch with it, you may find that you're ready to close the office, hang up the degree and become an artist or musician. Or you may discover that simply knocking off each day at 4:30 to engage in the hobby you love is enough to keep your batteries fully charged. It's different for everyone.

Simply said, following your passion doesn't have to mean chucking your career to this point. I have a client who has a heating and air conditioning company, but his passion is helping men create better lives for themselves. So he's creating a coaching business on the side, and while he's growing it, he's continuing to run his heating and AC company. He's doing what he's good at, but not passionate about, to enable him to gradually move toward what he is passionate about.

If you love your job but not your position, use your passion to create the opportunity to move to another position. Or to change companies. Or to refocus your existing career in another direction. I know attorneys who, once they made their money, left the meat grinder of corporate law behind to do nothing but environmental law and pro bono work for non-profits. Same career, but a passion-centered direction.

Wouldn't it be wonderful if corporate leaders embraced the concept of building business around their passions, and then let that filter down to the rank and file? Such companies would hire people not based on the holes in the management flowchart, but based on their passions. They would manage people not to prevent mistakes, but to bring out the greatness that lies in their passions. Executives would hold titles like Chief Passion Officer. Creativity would be encouraged and rewarded, and instead of leaving to start new companies, innovative employees would launch new business units based on ideas bred by untrammeled passion. That would revolutionize the workplace.

Unfortunately, if you're waiting around for your company, practice or industry to adopt such an approach to doing business, pack a lunch. It's going to be a while. But instead of waiting, you can take steps to move your profession closer and closer to your passion. Do it soon, because as another of my Passion Principles states:

> *If you don't define your passion,*
> *someone else will define it for you.*

Which would you prefer?

"Oh, It's Stupid!"

I'm psychic. I can predict with 90 percent accuracy what people will say in response to a particular question. The question is, "What's your passion?" I ask that of every person I coach and everyone who attends my speeches and presentations; it's the core of what I talk about. And almost every time, when people who are talking to me one-on-one hear that question, they shuffle their feet, roll their eyes and tell me their passion is stupid.

That's how we ended up here! These people have been told their passion is stupid so often that they begin to believe it. Americans are a Puritan people at heart; we distrust what our gut tells us in a way that many Europeans don't. Our culture is suspicious of passion as a motive for building a career. We'd much rather have hard-headed practicality as our prime mover. But while practicality is important, it doesn't breed passionate movers and shakers. It breeds drones. That brings up another Passion Principle:

> *Creativity will be attacked by passionless people.*

It's creative pursuits that are assaulted most often by our society's obsession with herding everyone into the ghetto of the practical. When young people, puffed up with idealism and artistic fire, announce their intention to go to college to become actors, writers or musicians, what do they almost always hear from well-meaning family? That they should take some sensible courses "so they have something to fall back on." Let me tell you, "something to fall back on" quickly becomes "something to fall into." Escape becomes hopeless. This attitude opens the door for failure, because it basically says to the creative person: "I don't think you have what it takes, so you should prepare to fall on your face."

When you are pursuing your passion, you've got to resist people's best intentions. Those who are not in touch with their passions can't see how you can build a career based on yours; all they see is the conventional path to earning a living, and passion often leads you on a path that's very different. The naysayers are truly afraid for you... and probably just a little envious. Because if you manage to do what you love and make a life out of it, what does that say about them?

Here's a guideline to follow: when other people tell you you're crazy, you're probably on the right path to your passion. Walt Disney had a scintillating vision for Disneyland, but he went bankrupt multiple times trying to bring it to fruition, because everybody (and I mean everybody) told him his idea was insane. He had to mortgage everything he owned to raise the money to build the park. Walt Disney was proven right because the only voice he listened to was the voice of his passion.

Let's Go Shopping

Here's an example of someone who thought her passion was stupid. I was speaking at an event for the Department of Social Services, and afterwards I found myself talking with a woman who appeared to be at her wit's end. I asked her what I ask everybody: "What's your passion?" She got that embarrassed look I know so well and said, "It's stupid." But I pressed her. "What do you love to do?"

Finally she told me. She loved to go shopping. What I did next made all the difference. Where most people probably rolled their eyes or laughed when she told them she loved to shop, I took her seriously. "OK, what do you like to shop for?" Gradually I wrung the facts from her: she loved to shop for clothing, she loved to shop with other women, and she was a smart, savvy shopper.

Finally, I asked her the million-dollar question. "What if you could build a business out of taking women shopping?" Her eyes positively glowed at the suggestion, and more than that, we had drawn a crowd of interested, attentive women. I suggested that she could create a small business in which she would take a group of women shopping in a limousine for perhaps $75 each, and throw in lunch for a little more. She could help them make wise purchases and find great deals and create a social circle for women who craved the company and camaraderie. Now my small audience of women was buzzing, and I told my budding entrepreneur that she had better start taking notes.

She grabbed paper and a pen and began writing down all the ideas I had given her. And what do you think happened? Her obvious passion for the idea flowed through the entire group of women standing around her, and they were immediately giving her more ideas for marketing, sales, services she could offer and the like. What had been a moribund group of stressed-out women a few minutes before was now an entrepreneurial think tank. It was one of the most wonderful things I've ever seen.

A few months later, it got better. I received a business card in the mail from the woman I had spoken with. She had started her shopping excursion business, had already taken her first group out, and had a second group scheduled. With passion, creativity and work, she had created a career she loved out of the activity she adored.

Love Your Failures

We've been taught to conceal our passions and not to believe in them for one simple reason: fear of failure. Following your passion is inherently risky; when you walk the path of passion you defy those who walk only where life is safe and predictable. You know the drill: pay attention in school, date the right girl (or guy), get your degree, say your prayers, get married, buy a house, pop out a kid or two, take your two weeks a year, vote, retire, play golf, die, amen. People who follow that path might never suffer any catastrophic failures, but they will also never know the white-hot elation of creating something from nothing, changing the lives of others, or touching spirits with a song, a poem or a sculpture.

Passion in your professional life means risk—but what is the greater risk? That you'll fall on your face doing something bold and original? Or that you'll sit in your comfort zone, deny your passion, and wind up whispering that terrible phrase, "I wish I would have..." on your deathbed? The risk of failing is infinitely more desirable than the risk of never trying. Wise people who walk the path of passion regard failure not as an end point, but as a rest stop. If you're fueled by passion, no failure is going to stop you; you're going to learn from your mistakes, change your strategy, and get back on the road.

In fact, as you move toward discovering and developing your passion in your work, you're going to find that failure is your friend. Passion is like clay; you never know how durable it is until it's put in the fire. In your journey toward a passion-centered career, you're going to hit roadblocks; they will open your eyes. If a failure discourages you, then perhaps what you thought was your passion isn't. If you've made mistakes, a failure is your chance to discover and correct them.

Being a passion-centered professional doesn't mean losing your fear. Fear reminds us we're alive. It's the canary in the coal mine that tells us we're taking a step outside our comfort zone, into the realm where we can produce real change in our lives. Following your passion simply means refusing to let fear stop you from taking the risks that each of us must take to bring our passion to life. And it's life—really living—that we're talking about.

Step One: Write Them Down!

Interesting stuff, Gary, but what does it have to do with my profession? How can all this help me stop hating what I do for a living? The answer is very simple. Now that you have an understanding of what passion is, what it does and how you lost track of yours, we're going begin a journey to help you relocate it. You're going to dig up that buried passion, nurture it, and discover ways to integrate it into your career at a level that allows you to make a living while loving what you do every day. Does that sound like something you're ready to do?

The first step is easy. In fact, it's so easy that the people I speak before are usually surprised when I ask them to do it. You see, hardly anyone has ever done it. *Write down the things you're passionate about.* Take out a piece of paper right now and write out a list of hobbies, causes, activities or ideas that own a piece of your soul, that get you excited just talking about them. Most people have never taken the time to do this, which may not be a big deal when you're in grade school and have all the time in the world to think about what you want to be when you grow up. But when you're an adult with a million demands from mortgage payments to car repairs intruding on your mind, you need to write things down.

Go ahead. Write down your passions, keeping these four rules in mind:

1. Nothing is stupid. Don't edit yourself.

2. Don't worry about which is most important.

3. Don't worry about writing down passions that you think apply to your career. You don't know what will affect your career right now.

4. Don't write down things you think you're "supposed" to be passionate about, like fine art or classical music. If you love fast food and '80s pop, write them down.

Writing down your passions is the most important first step toward discovering that single passion that will become the center of your professional life. In my experience, what you speak has only a 6-10 percent chance of coming to pass, while the same idea written down comes to pass 60-80 percent of the time. That's huge! When you write something down, you define it in a way you can't when it's an abstract thought. Written ideas give you focus and power. Start writing, and try to write down 25 things that fire your emotion and imagination.

A Few Examples For Your Passion List

- I have a passion for traveling with no particular destination.

- I have a passion for meeting new people.

- I have a passion for watching my son learn.

- I have a passion for living by the ocean.

- I have a passion for building perfectly functioning teams of good people.

- I have a passion for Bordeaux.

- I have a passion to play golf with friends who don't take it seriously.

- I have a passion to see the gorillas of the Congo up close.

- I have a passion to have my own radio show.

- I have a passion to dance the tango with my spouse.

- I have a passion for building computers out of spare parts.

- I have a passion for the sound of rain.

- I have a passion for creating beautiful indoor living spaces.

- I have a passion for volunteering to do scientific work overseas.

- I have a passion for hometown politics.

- I have a passion for studying the best minds in my profession.

- I have a passion to visit the temples of Cambodia.

- I have a passion to meet Nelson Mandela.

- I have a passion for fresh peaches taken right from the tree.

- I have a passion to savor every day with the people I love.

What does your passion list look like? It's probably a messy, chaotic blend of raw emotions, childhood dreams, grown-up aspirations and concrete goals. In other words, it's perfect. The purpose of making a list is to put you in touch with the many ways in which passion touches your life—to open your eyes to the fact that no matter how dead you think your passion might be, it's just lying quietly, waiting for you to shake it awake.

My Promise to You

From here, we're going to begin our journey in earnest, a journey to help you rediscover the passion that will transform your working life into a life that brings you delight, opportunity and limitless ability to transcend what you *thought* were your limitations. Because guess what? When you're working from passion, you have no limits, my friend.

In the coming chapters, I'm going to help you:

1. Dig up that buried passion or find a new passion.

2. Develop your passion into the driving force for your life.

3. Create ways to combine that passion with your profession so every day feels like Saturday and you're more successful—by any measure—than ever before.

Michelangelo was asked once how he had created his sublime, magnificent statue of David. His response: "I simply chipped away everything that was not David." We're going to chip away at everything that isn't your passion until we find the you that you were meant to be, hidden underneath… the you who lives and works with élan and courage and love and contemplation. The professional you've always wanted to be.

This is my promise to you: by the end of our time together I will give you the insight and tools you need to reveal the *emotion* that defines your passion, harness the *commotion* of your thoughts to use your passion productively, and develop the *devotion* to commit to whatever career path your passion leads you down. Because I can also promise you this: if you listen to your passion, even if it leads you away from where you thought you belonged into strange new territory, you will always end up where you're meant to be.

Passion Principles From This Chapter:

> *If your passion isn't part of what you do,*
> *you will never be rich.*

> *To build a career around passion*
> *is to live without regret.*

Your passion for life creates your position in life.

*If you don't define your passion,
someone else will define it for you.*

Creativity will be attacked by passionless people.

Chapter Two

The Nuts and Bolts of Passion

Passion impels our deeds; ideology supplies the explanations.
—Mason Cooley, U.S. aphorist

When I talk about passion, people will often hold up a hand and ask me, "Gary, what exactly is passion?" Good question, and one worth answering, so that's how we will spend this chapter.

Every passion starts with emotion. It's something in your life that defies reason. It just feels like something that you can't get out of your mind. There's no rhyme or reason for the intensity of how you feel when you hear a guitar playing, watch a teacher in front of her class or see a master woodworker making a rocking chair in his Appalachian workshop. You just know that something inexplicable about that thing speaks to the innermost part of your soul and fascinates you.

But here's where most people fall short: they base the pursuit of their passion entirely on that intense emotion. That won't work, because passion is always tested by opposition. In fact, I would say the greater your passion in life, the more challenging your life is destined to become. One of the lessons I try to teach my audiences and my coaching clients is that discovering your passion is not an easy journey, though it is a marvelous journey.

Small Minds and Mean Souls

It's almost a natural law that the further you go afield from the conventional way of doing things, the more other people will try to bring you down. Human behavior tends to revert to the mean—as Stephen King said in his review of the horror genre, *Danse Macabre*, we're always "watching for the mutant." The vast majority of human beings will never pursue their passion—who knows why? Laziness, fear, procrastination... there are as many reasons as people. But because they lack the courage to go after what might make their lives joyous and incredible, jealousy will often move them to prevent you from going for your passion. Chasing your passion turns you into a nail, and some folks like nothing better than to be hammers.

Individuals of small mind and mean soul may try to talk you out of your passion pursuit or derail you in some way. Most often, their assaults will be subtle: insinuating conversation like, "You're not really going to try that, are you?" or "You know, I knew a guy who did that once and he lost everything." Many times, it's the people closest to you who end up doing the hammering. The reason is simple: we're all reflections of one another, and when we see someone who's living 100 percent in her passion and knows who she is and why she's on this earth, the reflection shows us how we've failed to walk that same path. It reminds us that we've lacked the courage or drive to claim our birthright in life.

That's not going to be you. After all, you're reading this book. I'm going to share with you the underpinnings of passion—the ideas and processes that govern it. Once you know them, you'll understand how to shape your emotions and responses so you'll be immune to the jealousy of others and more focused on your journey toward the thing that turns your life into a wondrous adventure.

The Three Parts of Passion

Passion isn't a feeling at all. It's a process of taking your initial emotion and turning it into the active, evolving core of your life. Once you understand this, it's easier to look at passion as something you have to work on, rather than just something you experience. In reality, passion has three components:

Emotion—Feelings: what we exercise

Commotion—Thoughts: what we examine

Devotion—Commitment: what we execute

We've already talked about Emotion. Emotion will always be the starting point of the passion process, when you feel so intensely about a certain life direction, pursuit or purpose that you just can't get it out of your mind. It's here that something within you picks your life's unspoken rationale out of the flotsam and jetsam of options and ideas that bombard you on a daily basis. Why does one person steeped in years of medical school decide he can't live without chucking it all and becoming a steel sculptor? What makes a twelve-year-old girl adopt, seemingly out of nowhere, a bulldog determination to design eco-friendly buildings? Nobody knows, but it all begins with irresistible emotion.

With emotion, the key is paying attention. Don't shut out that siren song that may make no sense to you, but haunts your dreams. When the feeling that foreshadows your life's passion comes along, your only duty is to *listen to it*. Don't dismiss it or call it stupid. Give it a fair hearing. If you don't, you may never know whether or not it's pulling you in the direction that will change your life forever.

Commotion

When you listen to the intense emotions your passion produces and start thinking about what they mean to you, the result is Commotion. Commotion is the fast-paced thought process you experience as you begin contemplating what your passion might mean for you. What is your mind saying to you about how you're feeling? "No, this is crazy" is a common first thought, and for many people, the last thought on the subject. They just put it out of their minds, and their passions lie buried for good.

For those who continue past the self-doubt, other thoughts arise. Your interior voice might starting asking if this emotion is really important, and another voice might answer, "Of course it is, you schmuck." Early on, this is your self-editing process, your mind's way of trying to tune out thoughts that disrupt the status quo. You see, your rational mind doesn't want to change the patterns of your current life. It detests change and upheaval. It's the conservative, Apollonian side of yourself that tells you to get a good job, settle down, vote in every election and always wear a tie.

But passion isn't rational. It's the chaotic, Dionysian aspect of your psyche that wants you to let your passion loose to party hearty and see what happens. For most people, it's an act of heavy lifting to let that side of themselves go and see where it takes them. But if your goal is to pursue your passion where it leads, then it's vital that you turn off that internal editor and stop trying to talk yourself out of what you're feeling.

Ask yourself whom you're allowing to speak into your commotion. What voices are you hearing in your life? What people are whispering in your ear, and what are they saying? Your relationships will go a long way toward determining whether you follow or abandon your passion. When you're listening to your own emotions and you share them with the people in your life, what do you get in return? Doubt? Discouragement? Hope? Encouragement? At some point, you'll have to decide what kinds of relationships you'll allow in your passion-centered life.

One absolutely crucial point in dealing with the commotion stage:

Write your thoughts down.

Write down what you're feeling and thinking so that even when you're in doubt or you forget what was coursing through your cerebrum, you can go back and look at what was happening in your mind in the heat of the moment. Passion Principle:

> *Revisit.*
> *Retool.*
> *Re-examine.*
> *Experience a renaissance.*

The beauty of writing down your thoughts and feelings when you're in the commotion period is that the act of writing them makes them real. Suddenly, your passion is more than an abstraction—it's factual. There's a record of it. You can speculate and make notes and daydream and plan. You're a step closer to making this crazy idea a real part of your life.

Devotion

Finally, there's Devotion, which is what you do to execute your plan and bring your passion to life. Feelings are what we exercise in Emotion; thoughts are what we analyze in Commotion. In devotion, we get our butts out of bed, put our tennis shoes on, ignore the part of our minds that scream, "What are you doing? It's 5:30 in the morning!" and run to train for our marathon. Devotion means ignoring all the reasons why you can't make this passion a reality and doing what you have to do anyway.

Just showing up every day and doing what has to be done—that's devotion. No passion comes to life overnight. If you expect it to, you'll set yourself up for disappointment. Think of your life as an ocean liner trying to turn at sea: no matter how hard you throw the helm over, it's going to take some time for that massive vessel to change course. Adopting a new hobby and becoming proficient at it can take months. Changing careers can take years.

Creating that perfect painting or novel can take decades. Passion Principle:

> *Realizing your passion will take time,*
> *diligence and patience.*

This is one of my favorite examples of this principle. I was in Miami and I saw an elderly couple down by the pool. I walked down to them and said, "Excuse me, can I ask you a question?" The gentleman, who had to be in his 80s, had a great sense of humor, because he looked at me and said, "Hurry up."

I asked, "How long have you been married?" And as soon as I asked the question you could see the passion for his wife light up the man's eyes. He grabbed her hand tightly and said, "We've been married for sixty years."

"Let me ask you," I said, "what's the key to staying married that long?" He looked at me a long time, as if wondering why I was so nosy, and then said, "When I wanted to quit and not be married anymore, I didn't go by what I felt for her. I didn't even go by what I knew. I went by the commitment that I made to her sixty years ago. The feeling, that's just the dessert that comes after all the pain."

Isn't that fantastic? Love, as they say, is a choice, not a feeling. Well, passion is not a feeling, but a choice. Part of the devotion stage is understanding that in the process of bringing your passion to life, you are going to have days when you say, "To heck with it. What was I thinking?" You're going to have down times when you want to quit and go back to your anesthetized life. Often, people will give up just before they're going to make it, which kills me to see.

You can't get to the summit without going through the valleys. When you're making radical changes to how you work, think and live, you're going to descend into some deep valleys and wonder how you'll get out. But remember, the deeper the valley, the higher the mountain. The valleys are where your character is shaped, while the mountaintops are where the vision is cast. If you're going to bring that fiery emotion of passion to your profession, know that it will take unflagging dedication.

The Three Kinds of Vision

Notice how everything in this book comes in threes? I think that's because there are three kinds of people in life:

1. Those who are living in their passion.

2. Those who are in the process of making their passion a reality.

3. Those who have buried their passions.

We're concerned here with the second group, and the next aspect of bringing your passion to life is understanding the three kinds of vision that define how we live:

1. Tunnel Vision—Exhausted and used up; moving past passion

2. Nonell Vision—Exiting and giving up; moving away from passion

3. Funnel Vision—Energized and built up; moving toward passion

Tunnel Vision

When you have Tunnel Vision, all you can see is what's in front of you. You're living with your head down and your nose pressed against the grindstone, never looking up to see what else is possible. You're tired and don't know why, unhappy and can't see the reason. Think of two parallel lines, like those in the graphic on the next page:

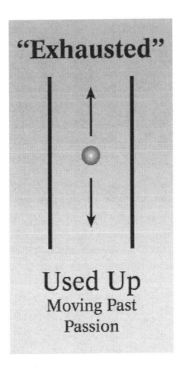

When you're seeing with Tunnel Vision, you might be passing by your passion every day. Or you might know what it is but be convinced the time isn't "right" to chase after it. This is common. I hear people all the time who say, "I know what my passion is, I know what I want to do, and when I get enough time and money, I'm going to do it." Or, "When the weekend comes, I'm going to do what my passion is." Of course, those people never end up making their passions happen.

People with Tunnel Vision aren't hopeless cases, they're just people who need awakening. You may have been one of them before you opened this book, but hopefully the material you've seen so far has helped you raise your head and see that you are only locked into the life you have today if you allow yourself to be. When you have that epiphany, you're on your way to:

Funnel Vision

Here, you've realized what your passion is and you're in the process of focusing, paring away the unnecessary aspects of life until all that's left is that part of you that you simply must shout to the heavens. Part of bringing your passion to life is throwing overboard all the things that aren't your passion and engaging in the *one thing* that gives you the most joy and meaning. Think of it as two lines rising and converging, like this:

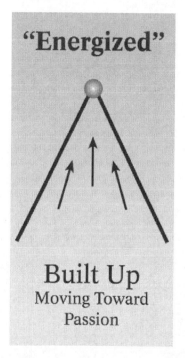

"Energized"

Built Up
Moving Toward
Passion

When you see with Funnel Vision, you're continually narrowing your field of view. You're not becoming narrow-minded, but you are learning to differentiate the distractions of your life from the energies, people and work that form the heart of that thing you were meant to do. Like Billy Crystal says in the film *City Slickers*, you're thinking about "one thing, just one thing." It's going from finding your way by flashlight to finding your way by laser. Both put out the same energy but have very different effects!

Nonell Vision

People with Nonell Vision are the ones who've given up. They don't want to know about passion and don't care what they're missing. They are moving away from their passions and into a life of vagueness, entropy and uncertainty. Picture a visual field that looks like two lines moving away from each other as they go upward:

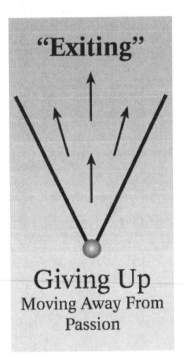

People with Nonell Vision are in effect saying, "I'm going to let everybody else define my passion." They become resentful, bitter, angry and burnt out because they're not doing what they were really called to do. They do what they hate for 30 years… and they blame everybody else. That's a tragedy. I met a dentist in Arizona who was making big money. But when I asked him, "What's your passion?" he said, "I have absolutely no idea. I just know dentistry isn't it."

You don't have to worry about Nonell Vision, because just by picking up this book you've proven that you see there's more than your current life and career. But what about your friends or family? Is someone you know living life unfulfilled and miserable without even knowing why? Such people can think they're immune to the power of passion, when in reality their passion is just so deeply buried that it takes a heroic effort to uncover it.

Life Levels—How Are You Living?

I was speaking in Phoenix, and next door to the office of the gentleman I was speaking for was an orthodontist's office. My client told me, "You need to talk to this guy." So I went over, and when I walked into his office... wow. All over his office he had professionally displayed about a million dollars' worth of classic electric guitars, autographed by the likes of Jimi Hendrix and the Eagles. The place looked like the Hard Rock Café. Then I went into some of his exam rooms and... more wow. One was a ski room, done up completely in ski gear and ski artwork, very tasteful and classy. Another was a Hawaii room—and I'm not talking cheeseball Don Ho at the tiki lounge stuff, but first-rate Polynesian décor.

This gentleman was a very successful, very wealthy orthodontist, but his success had given him the freedom to explore passions like guitars, skiing and travel to Hawaii, and this was his way of bringing those passions with him to his work. He wasn't about to retire at this stage of his career and become a beach bum or ski bum, but he could bring the feeling of those passions with him every day to his office.

That brings us to the concept of Life Levels. Like the three types of vision, Life Levels are metrics that allow you to look at the life you're currently leading and gauge how much of your passion you are bringing into it. Everything in this chapter is really just a method for understanding where your head is at—how you're thinking and feeling about your life and your passion. Once you get an idea of whether you're at the Emotion, Commotion or Devotion stage, and once you know whether you've been living with

Tunnel, Funnel or Nonell vision to this point, you can step back and say to yourself, "OK, this is the Life Level I'm at today."

Knowing your Life Level tells you what you need to do and how far you have to go to really embrace and realize your passion in your daily life. The five levels are like mileage signs on a highway that read, "Your Passion: 186 miles. Gas/food/lodging." The concept of Life Levels is important because of another Passion Principle:

> *Progress toward your passion won't be consistent.*

You'll have good days and bad days. You'll make progress, then fall back. If your passion is strong enough, you'll take two steps forward for every step back, but you're human. We all falter sometimes in our move toward bigger and better things. Remember, bringing your passion to life is *change*, and change is never easy. Even if the way you choose to express your passion is simple, like the orthodontist with the guitars and Hawaiian room, staying motivated through a period of change isn't simple. Think of running a marathon. It's simple: just run for 26 miles without stopping. But easy? I don't think so. That's why people train for months and years to run them. So to really twist a metaphor, think of Life Levels as those people with the cups of Gatorade along the side of the race route, encouraging you and reminding you that you can make it to the finish.

All Right Already... What are the Life Levels?

Sorry, sometimes I get carried away in my enthusiasm. These are the five Life Levels. They represent not just your type of vision or your feelings, but your entire existence: job, health, happiness, finances, all of it.

Level 1: You're completely unaware of what your passion is or that you even have one. You're miserable but you don't know why. You didn't even know what it was to have a passion until you started reading this book, and you didn't even want to do that until your friend blackmailed you (kidding!). This is where most people reside, and it's an ugly neighborhood. As quickly as you can, you need to escape to:

Level 2: Level Two is where you have not done anything about your passion yet, but you know it exists. You're beyond Tunnel Vision and you've done the basic self-examination of Commotion. You've thought about what your passion might be, you've admitted that you're unhappy, and you're becoming aware of the many ways in which unexpressed passion is impacting your life in a negative way. You're becoming more self-aware, but not taking any action yet.

Level 3: Here, you're starting to make plans. You've probably written down your passion and in a fever of excitement starting scribbling wild ideas and schemes, ranging from chucking your current career and moving to a Tibetan monastery to changing the wallpaper in your office. That's great! Forward motion is always wonderful. Remember, don't edit yourself. Brainstorm. Dream. Make plans, and don't worry about how wild they are. Just know that in the end, moving beyond Level 3 means you eventually need to make some realistic plans that you can actually carry forward, with specific action steps, timelines and so on. You should come out of this with a blueprint for embracing your passion.

Level 4: This is an exciting level, because you have your plan and you're taking action to realize your passion. Bravo! The action might be in the early stages, where you're doing research or saving money. Or it might be in the radical stage, where you've quit your job and launched your own business. It doesn't matter. You're doing something that perhaps *five percent* of all human beings on this earth will ever do: listening to the voice in your soul, following your heart and making something great happen. This level can last six months or six years.

Level 5: You don't need me to tell you what this level is. Here, you're living your passion daily. You made it. You're one of the lucky ones. You started your company, joined a rock band, got into that hobby you've loved since you were a kid, changed careers or transformed your company from the inside. You love your life and approach every day with new energy and optimism. Heck, you're my hero! Best of all, other people see how you radiate passion and ask you, "What did you do?" And you get to share your story with them. How cool is that?

The Life Levels give you hope, don't they? They're a reminder that it's not all that far from Level 1 to Level 5. All it takes is awareness and motivation. That brings on a Passion Principle:

> *You can skip Life Levels if you're really motivated.*

You don't have to plod from one to five. If your vision for your passion and your life is so white-hot and overpowering, maybe you jump in a day from Level 1, where you're not even thinking about passion, to Level 5, where you're taking instant action and seeing instant results. It can be that easy to change your life. Think about what level you're living at, and how you can get to the next one. That's how lasting change happens—step by persistent step!

A Choice, Not a Chance

What I'm really talking about here is attitude. Your attitude is how you explain the events of life. Either you're explaining them in a positive way, or you're putting most of life in the negative column. Which way you choose determines so much.

Let me tell you a little story. A few years back my wife Cherisse asked me to come somewhere with her, but she wouldn't tell me where. "If I tell you, you won't do it," she said. *Danger, Will Robinson, danger.* I regarded this lovely yet indomitable woman with all the husbandly patience I could muster.

"Beverly Hills," she said.

Okay, that wasn't so bad. I've always enjoyed my time there: fine dining, shopping, star watching. Cool. But there was more. "We're going to a place called Slimmins."

"Slimmins?"

She broke into a grin, because I obviously had no idea what this place was. I was prepared to protest, and then she cheated. She said, "It would mean a lot to me." Rats. Those words were like kryptonite, and she knew it. So we were off to Beverly Hills. Upon arrival, I noted to my horror that Slimmins was not a restaurant. In fact, it might be the exact opposite of a restaurant. Slimmins is Richard Simmons' workout studio! My first exercise move was a nicely executed 180-degree turn (in the pike position, no less) back toward the parking lot. I mean, I could sense the anti-macho in the building.

I pled, "Please don't make me go in there! Please don't make me work out with Richard Simmons!" I insisted that this was a mistake, that Richard wouldn't even be there in person anyway. Cherisse was having none of it. She's a Simmons fanatic, with the tapes, meals and sweatbands to prove it. Her positive attitude didn't falter for a second in the face of my sniveling. Finally, because I knew how much it meant to her, I followed her in. But I was determined not to enjoy it.

The first thing I noticed was that there were hardly any men. Great. But there were a lot of women in Spandex—rows of them, arranged like Roman legionnaires, stamping like horses in the starting gate before a race. Cherisse grabbed me and—horrors!—dragged me to the front of the room, the last place I wanted to be. I was looking for a place to hide when suddenly thumping music began, a ripple went through the crowd, and Richard Simmons himself came bounding into the room, clad in his trademark tank top and waving his arms like a rock star. I took this as my cue to slip quietly to the back of the room.

Once there, I waved one arm limply to the beat so it would look like I was exercising. I kept my eyes glued to my watch. I radiated grumpy disinterest during the first five minutes of the workout. I wanted to be shopping on Rodeo Drive. I wanted to be at the Hollywood Bowl. I wanted to be stuck in L.A. traffic. Anywhere but there.

Then I glanced up from my watch for a second and found my view blocked by an enormous head of frizzy hair. Much to my surprise, Richard Simmons himself was standing nose to nose with me!

"I want you to know something, mister!" he screeched. "You're bringing everybody in this gym down, and if you want to work it, your attitude had better change! If you want to stay here, you've got to have a positive mental attitude, because these women are working *hard*, do you understand me? If you're going to stay here, WORK IT!" And with this he began pumping my arms and yelling, "Work it! Work it! Work it!"

I went from the blackest, darkest attitude to doing the Pony in three seconds flat, and it was at that moment I realized that we all have the power to change our attitude. It can happen in a moment's time. Attitude is a *choice*, not a *chance*.

The Tipping Point

I know a guy who was going along just great in his early 40s, kind of healthy but not ever realizing that he had been gaining a little weight every year until he was about 60 pounds overweight. He didn't exercise much, and he ate OK, but not spectacularly. Then one day he went into his doctor for a routine physical and found out that he had very high blood pressure. Well, you'd think this guy had been shot out of a gun. He immediately started on an intense exercise regimen, changed his diet to where he was eating vegetarian 90 percent of the time, and lost 65 pounds in eight months. He made a permanent, instant lifestyle change, and he's now the healthiest he's ever been in his entire life.

He'd reached his "tipping point." The tipping point is a concept made popular by the book *The Tipping Point*, by Malcolm Gladwell, but it's been around for years. The basic idea is, change doesn't happen immediately, but small motivators for change accumulate in a person, a city or a company, unseen and unnoticed, like drops of liquid into a cooking pot. Each of them moves people or institutions imperceptibly closer and closer to the point where they are ready to take radical action. Then one significant thing happens and *boom*! The pot overfills, tips over and a flood of extreme change ensues.

That's what happened with my friend. Small things—not feeling great, some family health issues, aging knees—had slowly piled up to the point where, when he heard his blood pressure numbers, he said, "That's it. I'm taking control of this today." And he did. There was no gradual change. He amputated his old lifestyle and grew a new one. Again, we see the importance of attitude. A negative attitude would have meant denial and anger. But with a positive attitude, he was able to see hope and make that hope a reality.

Your Point of KNOW Return

I bring this up because to make the lasting changes that will bring your passion to the center of your life, you have to be at your own personal tipping point. Becoming a passion-centered professional doesn't happen when everything is hunky-dory; if you're deliriously happy with your work and your life, why would you change anything? It happens when times are difficult. You can have your personal epiphany about your life and make all the lists in the world, but (and this is a Passion Principle):

> *Life-altering change comes not when things are easy, but when the environment is difficult.*

Changing your career to serve some fiery inner vision is rarely simple. You're going to feel fear. People are going to tell you that you're crazy. Family members and colleagues will be angry with you. You might worry about losing your house or your business.

Who knows? But when things are hard and you can't take your current life any longer, that's when it's essential that you take action and stick with it.

Because difficulty and change go hand in hand, you've got to be ready to take big, bold steps in your life. To do that, you've got to get to what I call the *Point of KNOW Return*. It's the same idea as the tipping point concept, but more original and more evocative, I think. The Point of KNOW Return is when something happens that makes your mind instantly speak up and say, "That's it! I can't take it anymore! I'm going to do something about this right now, today!" You KNOW your passion is screaming, you KNOW you have to take action, and you might even KNOW what your first step is.

That's awesome. When you hit the Point of KNOW Return, don't think. Just feel and do. Don't rationalize yourself out of it, or you might lose the moment. Follow your gut and you'll amaze yourself. This is the point of no turning back. Following your passion is no longer an idle conversation, but a visceral *need* in your gut. You might quit your job tomorrow or fly to Europe. Who knows? Do it. Even if it's not exactly in the direction of your final passion destination, taking instant, passion-fueled action will let you know it's possible... and it will make you feel incredible and empowered.

Listen or Regret

Later in this book, we'll talk about specific steps and processes that will help you turn your Point of KNOW Return into focused action and progress. But know this: you may have no control over what will bring you to that point. Little things may have been piling up inside you for years without your knowledge, and one more bad day at the office may be enough for you to say, "This is it." On the other hand, you'll never see your Point of KNOW Return unless you're looking for it. So it's essential that you start becoming aware of your feelings about your life—and not dismissing them, but really listening to what your mind and spirit are telling you.

Personally, I don't think you can create your own Point of KNOW Return. It just happens, and it's different for every one of us. However, I do think that like in many other areas of life, you can put yourself in the right position to receive that awareness when it does arrive. As baseball legend Branch Rickey said, "Luck is the residue of design." There are things you can do to make your mind a full pot that the Point of KNOW Return is ready to tip over:

1. Take some risks in the direction of your passion. If you know what you want but can't get yourself to make the leap, dip your toe in the water. If starting a business in your passion, go to a weekend trade show involving that business. Talk to people. Make contacts. Commit to something you're not ready to do, then be forced to do it. Get out on the tightrope and you'll be amazed at how alive you'll feel.

2. Start listening to yourself. What is your inner monologue saying about your situation? Do you keep having the thought, "I've got to get out of this situation"? Why? Do you listen, or do you immediately tell yourself to shut up and stop behaving like a child? Instead, start listening to what your inner voice is saying. Keep a journal.

3. Be ready to act when your Point of KNOW Return comes. Be self-aware enough to know that "something" just happened that turned your world upside down, and seize the moment. It's out of your control to make the moment appear, but when it does, you need to respond. As author Chuck Swindell said, "Life is ten percent about what happens to you and 90 percent about how you *respond* to what happens to you." Be aware, and when the opportunity comes, grab it. Be ready to take a risk and have your perception of your own capacities transformed. That brings up a new Passion Principle:

> *It's amazing what you can do*
> *when you don't know what you can't do.*

I had a client once who wanted to make changes but whom I could not get off the bubble, because he simply was not able to listen to his inner voices and reach his Point of KNOW Return. He wanted me to coach him, and my coaching services are a considerable investment, because I only coach a selected number of people at a time. And while he would say all the right things, like "I need to go forward, this is exactly what I need," I knew he wasn't ready. He was trying to convince himself he was ready to overthrow everything in his mindset to pursue his passion, but he wasn't *feeling* it. When you're ready, you won't have to talk yourself into anything. You'll KNOW.

Fear Itself

In the end, the greatest obstacle to pursuing your passion is the greatest obstacle in life: fear. Inertia, a refusal to listen to one's inner voice, lack of confidence in your ability to take risks—all are the result of fear. What fear? Fear of failure, of appearing ridiculous to others, or of losing everything you've built so far, even though it's not making you happy. People who are aware that they have an unfulfilled passion but do nothing about it are usually paralyzed by fear.

However, fear can be your best friend if you embrace it and look at it from the proper perspective. Fear really comes from one thing: taking yourself out of your comfort zone. When you take a risk or move into an unknown territory, you get off well-trodden paths and into areas where you might lose money or the respect of others. But it's precisely when you're out of your comfort zone, scared to death half the time, that you're starting to live in your passion. It's funny, but fear is the thing that can motivate our passions, and fear is the thing that can kill them. It's all in how you handle fear!

Looked at with the proper perspective, fear is the force that can get you off the bubble and into action toward bringing your passion to life. If you're afraid that you'll be stuck for the next 30 years in a career situation you despise, that's pretty motivating. Fear can be a friend if you look at it according to this Passion Principle:

> *Nervous, uncomfortable fear is a sign that you're out of your comfort zone and into the territory of your passion.*

Fear is a great reminder that you're taking the risks you should. You shouldn't be terrified, but if you're filled with nervous energy and vibrating with excitement over the unknown, then it's likely that you're far out of your comfort zone and into an area where good, new things are likely to happen. Remember, passion is about making radical changes, and sometimes those changes will be un-nerving... at first. But soon, the changes will become exciting. When that happens, fear turns to exhilaration.

False Evidence Appearing Real

That's the definition of fear: False Evidence Appearing Real. Fear tells you things will never change, or that things are worse than they are, or that you don't have what it takes. But fear lies. That's its nature. Fear corrodes your will to find and realize your passion... if you let it. But channeled and used properly, fear can be the motiva-tor you need to get going.

Jim Rippey is a professional snowboarder, BASE jumper and daredevil. He's an incredible guy. His whole philosophy is based around responding to fear. He says that fear is a natural, healthy emotion, but that you have two choices in responding to it: you can let it control you, or you take can control of it and use it to reach your goals. Jim uses fear to keep him in prime physical condition and to make him prepare extremely well for his adventures, and that allows him to take risks and still be safe.

So, how are you facing your fear? If you're letting your fear control you, why? Are you happier because of it? Are you proud of yourself? Or do you realize that you need to quit being intimidated by the unknown and start facing the uncertainties that your passion implies? Life does not drop good things on your head. Life is like a fruit tree: you have to go get the fruit. And as a wise man once said, "Go out on a limb. That's where the fruit is." You'll never find your passion without facing your fear and taking risks. Once you can do that, you're unstoppable.

Focus

If I've been a little harsh in this chapter, I'm sorry. No, I'm not. Because discovering your passion-centered life takes guts and self-knowledge, and there's no softball path to those qualities. You need motivation and determination to make things happen for yourself. But you also need one more quality: *focus.*

Focus simply means that when you have all these other essentials in place—self-awareness, positive response to fear, risk taking and so on—what you finally need when your Point of KNOW Return comes is focus. When you reach the Life Level where you're aware of your passion and what you need to do to bring it to life, the emotions you'll experience will be overwhelming. You'll be regretful, frightened, angry, excited, energized and slightly insane. That's cool. But in the end, if you're going to make something happen, you've got to tame those feelings and move ahead in a focused direction.

You need plans. You need one goal. You can't chase after 25 passions. You've got to choose one and go after it with everything you have. Again, later on we'll go through a comprehensive series of exercises and processes that will get you there. But for now, just know that as exciting as the rush of passion and self-realization is —and it's a true epiphany that's unlike anything else you'll ever experience—it won't get you anywhere until you channel that feeling and refine it into clean, life-changing energy.

That's the idea I'd like to close this chapter with: you're a passion refinery. Silly, but it sticks with you, doesn't it? It's clean energy, with no carbon emissions, and the mileage you'll get out of it is infinite. Now let's move on and talk about how passion will impact your daily life.

Passion Principles in this chapter:

> *Revisit.*
> *Retool.*
> *Re-examine.*
> *Experience a renaissance.*

> *Realizing your passion will take time,*
> *diligence and patience.*

> *Progress toward your passion won't be consistent.*

> *You can skip Life Levels if you're really motivated.*

> *Life-altering change comes*
> *not when things are easy, but difficult.*

> *It's amazing what you can do*
> *when you don't know what you can't do.*

> *Nervous, uncomfortable fear is a sign that*
> *you're out of your comfort zone*
> *and into the territory of your passion.*

Chapter Three

Why Passion Matters in Your Life and Career

Without passion man is a mere latent force and possibility, like the flint which awaits the shock of the iron before it can give forth its spark.

—*Henri-Frédéric Amiel, Swiss philosopher and poet*

The pursuit of passion is all well and good, but we're also talking about your professional life. Whether you're a doctor, lawyer, financial advisor, architect, dentist, psychologist or one of a hundred other demanding professions, you can't help but ask yourself: "If I put all this time and effort into developing and living my passion, is it going to benefit my career? Or could I actually hurt my business and my earning power?"

The answer is, it depends. It depends what your passion is and how you go after it. I've made it clear that I'm not suggesting you have to dump your law practice and run off to Oahu's North Shore to become a surf bum; you can usually integrate your passion into your current work, if you want to. I suspect that's what most of the people who read this book will do: keep working in their chosen fields but adjust their working lives or their lives in general to accommodate their passions, which will become a part-time occupation. Some will cut back their work hours to devote more time to their passion. A few will retire early and do what they love. And a handful will close the book on their professional life and go into a completely different career that serves their passion. Again, it depends on the voice inside you.

But for now, let's look at the majority, the professionals who want to keep doing the work that has made them successful, but who also want to integrate their passion into that work. For them (and you if you're among them), it might seem a little futile to invest energy and time into nurturing your passion if it's not going to help your career. But it's not futile. In this chapter, I'm going to talk about some of the ways that integrating your passion into your work—and simply finding your passion in your life away from the office—will benefit your productivity, bottom line, and happiness.

The Guitar Man

In the last chapter, I told you about the orthodontist whose office was filled with beautifully mounted electric guitars, some signed by artists like Jimi Hendrix and probably worth more than a million dollars. He also had the Hawaii room and the downhill skiing room in his office. I talked to him about how this benefited him in his work, and he told me that he simply enjoyed coming to work more being in an environment that reminded him of the things he loved. That's one of the most essential benefits of bringing out your passion: you'll enjoy work and life more. It's elemental.

Then I asked him whether or not his expression of his passion had left any room for his team members to express theirs. You should have seen this man's face; it was as if a curtain had been lifted. He hadn't even thought about his staff. He got very silent, and then we talked about the question. It turned out that in all areas of his life, he was so passionate that his passions sometimes crowded out those of others. He thanked me for bringing that to light, and told me he would begin encouraging his team to express their own passions on the job.

The question of simply getting more joy out of your work seems so simple that many people miss it. But it's the most important benefit of becoming a passion-centered professional. We're not automatons; we're people. Ideally, we don't just go to work and slave away thoughtlessly in a cubicle, though many people do just that. But in the best of worlds, work is a part of a holistic life that's filled with stimulation, meaning and purpose—not every second (I defy you to find cosmic meaning in photocopying), but some of the time. Whether your passion is expressed at work or takes up most of your spare time when you're not at the office, when you're expressing your passion you feel more alive. You don't feel like a drone defined by your work. You feel alive. As a result, you do everything, including your job, better.

The Soccer Coach

Another example illustrates this beautifully. I do some intense coaching with a huge, bureaucratic public agency in California. Last year, they asked me to come in and meet with some of their employees to get a feel for their work, their concerns and so on. I walked into one manager's office after being told that he was very unhappy. In fact, he was looking for an exit strategy, because he was feeling burnt out and exhausted by his job. This is very common in the people I work with; they don't know what the problem is but they know they're not happy.

I walked into his office, and the first thing I noticed on his desk was a picture of a soccer team. Now, let me break off a second to talk about awareness and passion. I'm trained to notice indicators of people's passions because that's my focus. I'm almost like a lay psychologist whose attention is on passion and the expression of passion. I find that ninety percent of the time, people will give you clues about what their passions are, and I'm very good at spotting those clues. Where other people see office clutter, I see red flags labeled, "Hey genius, this is what I really care about!"

That was the case here. I asked the guy what the picture was, and he lit up like a Christmas tree. "That's my kid's soccer team," he said proudly. And I asked him more questions and found out that not only did his kid play soccer, but he coached the team! As he talked about it, his whole demeanor changed. Then I asked the $64,000 question: "You like coaching?"

"I *love* coaching," he replied. So I asked him, "Would you say that coaching soccer for you is a passion?" And he said, "If I could do nothing else, I would love to just coach kids' soccer." Jackpot. Turned out the guy had played semipro soccer, which nobody knew.

"So soccer is pretty much your life," I proposed. He grinned. "If I could, I would fill this office with soccer stuff." At this point, I knew I had what I needed to help this man turn things around. So I asked him about fundamentals that he taught his players, and he ran off a whole list for me, character-building concepts like "Come ready to play" and "Pass the ball, it's not all about you." The conversation went on for more than an hour, and the guy became more and more animated and energized. Then I asked him if he had ever written down some of the teaching tools he used for his soccer team with an eye on applying them to the people he supervised, and he said the thing I almost always hear when someone talks about their passion: "No, they're stupid."

There it was, that self-defeating phrase. That minimization of something near and dear to the human heart. It was my job to get this manager to understand that his passion was anything but stupid. I pointed out to him that he might think they were stupid, but the concepts he taught changed kids and helped them become a team. He agreed, and he continued sharing his coaching principles with me. I wrote them down in a list ten items long. Finally, he asked me, "Why are you writing this down?"

I told him, "I have some ideas. What if you used these same ten principles that you use with your soccer team as coaching concepts for your team here at work?"

Man, this cat came alive like you would not believe—sat up in his chair, slammed his hands down on his desk, and looked as if he'd just bitten into an electric wire. "I never thought of that!" he exclaimed. "Do you think they would even listen to them?"

I told him, "They would if the principles came from the point of your passion, not just your position." I knew that if he tried to cram his coaching ideas down the throat of his subordinates by virtue of being their superior, he would fail. But if he expressed that they were part of his consuming passion, that passion would resonate with the other people and they'd love every minute. Today, not only has this manager not quit, not only has he been meeting once a month with his team to talk about the soccer principles, but he's been asked to teach some of this coaching methods to other departments within the organization.

Passionauts

These are but two examples of hundreds of people I have met who are what I call *passionauts*. The Latin suffix "naut" means "voyager." So "astronaut" means "star voyager," and "passionaut" means "passion voyager." That's what you're doing by following the advice in this book: going on a voyage of discovery that's going to take you beyond the bounds of what society expects of you and the limitations you may have been placing on yourself. So you're a passionaut, too! Congratulations. Welcome to the fraternity of passion.

Some of the greatest people in the world are passionauts. Here are just a few who are living as I write this book (there are millions more who have passed on):

- Richard Branson

- Steve Jobs

- Quincy Jones

- Tipper Gore

- Al Gore

- Howard Schulz, founder of Starbucks

- Lance Armstrong

- Maya Angelou

- Nelson Mandela

- Steven Spielberg

- Oprah Winfrey

- Philippe Cousteau

- Billy Graham

- Jimmy Carter

- David Brashears, Everest climber

I'm sure I've missed hundreds of famous passionauts, and there are thousands upon thousands of people who are changing the world with their passion, but whom few people outside their specialized field have heard of. But fame isn't the point. Passion becomes mission, and mission becomes change that benefits not only you but the people around you, sometimes on a global scale. The people who founded this nation were passionauts. Be proud to be in their company.

People Respond to Passion

The moral of that rather long story is that when you bring something as fundamentally human into your work, other people will respond to it. The trouble is, we're taught to be "professional," which has come to mean impersonal and dispassionate. My mission is to break you of that conditioning and help you bring your passion into your work whenever and wherever it's appropriate and possible.

One of the basic benefits of bringing passion into your profession is that it makes you more human and shows people that you care about things other than your work. That implies something very important for the people you work with: *that you care about them.* That motivates. When people know that you care about their needs and their passions, they become more motivated to work harder for you, innovate, solve problems and inspire others. Nothing increases productivity like a feeling of being appreciated and valued for who you are.

If you're one of those bosses who simply don't care about their people—your attitude is, "You're here to work, you're here to get things done, you're here to make sure that the bottom line is taken care of, you're here to make me look good"—then what you're saying to people is, "I don't care about who you are, just what you do." You're telling people that they are their positions, and therefore replaceable. And as I've said, you cannot inspire based on your position, only your passion. Bosses and managers who make people feel like interchangeable parts end up with departments of lifeless zombies who will do just enough work not to get fired. That's our first Passion Principle for this chapter:

> *Passion increases company productivity.*

The Theft of Dignity

The beautiful thing about giving your organization a "passion transfusion" is that when you start making people know you care about them, they come alive. You can see it in their attitudes when they come to work, how they carry themselves, everything they do. You awaken their creativity. They show up on time and stay later to get things done. They make fewer mistakes on the job. Instead of taking long lunches to avoid their work, they come back on time and are actually excited to get to their jobs. In companies I've worked with, you even see the rumor mill slow down or shut down completely. There's no more gossip, because everyone feels valued and there's no need to snipe at each other to feel superior.

On the other side of the spectrum, the companies I've gone into that are on "passion life support" have an oppressive atmosphere. People hate to come to work. Absenteeism is high, workers have more health issues, and more mistakes occur, often leading to safety problems on the job. You have people stealing from the company because they just don't care. The unspoken creed in such places —whether they have ten employees or ten thousand—is *you don't give a hoot about us, so we're going to return the favor.* The company becomes "The Man." In the end, productivity plummets.

The sad truth is, I have never seen more lack of focus on human beings and their emotional needs that I do in the workplace today. I suspect it's part of the larger disease of our culture, in which emotional, mental and spiritual health is ignored in favor of quarterly earning reports and executive bonuses. I see it in the little things, like when someone is sharing something very personal with a colleague and that colleague is looking at her watch as if to say, "How much longer do I have to pretend to care?" That's an assault on the dignity of the person, and it happens every day.

The Gift of Your Attention

Which kind of practice, company or corporation would you rather have? If you're hidebound to old practices and can't shake the idea that showing your passion or letting your people know they are valued is "touchy-feely," then it might be time to begin looking at problems that affect you in your work (or your practice or company) and ask, "Why does this happen?" Because there are genuine benefits to passion. If you're a professional who expresses and supports passion in your workplace, bravo to you. If not, you've got a lot of company.

If you run a practice or company, what's the environment like with regard to listening to other people when they talk about things that are personally important to them? Is it respectful or impatient? Passion Principle:

Newly expressed passion is fragile.

When people are first expressing their passion, they're always tentative and worried about being seen as—repeat after me—"stupid." Their passion is like fine china: easily broken and hard to mend. I have a friend who has three incredible sons, all deeply into sports. When we have breakfast, the first thing he starts talking about are his sons and what they've been doing, and he comes to life. But what would happen if I started looking at my watch, or worse, said something like, "We're not really here to talk about your kids. There are other things I want to talk to you about"? I would shut him down completely. He would never bring up his kids again. It would ruin our relationship, make it cold and superficial.

Sometimes the best gift you can give anyone is your attention when they need it most. Let me share an example with you. Years ago, I was speaking to a group of students at a major university. After my presentation, they did what they usually do: gather around to ask questions. During this time I noticed a girl about nineteen out of the corner of my eye. She had been crying. When she came up to me she began to speak slowly and deliberately, but nothing could have prepared me for her words.

"The thirty-eight caliber revolver is under the pillow on my bed," she said. "I have written wills to all of my friends and relatives, and they are on my desk with some of my personal possessions. To-night I am going to go back to my dorm, point the gun at the roof of my mouth and pull the trigger. I am so tired of living like this."

What if, as she was telling me this story, I had simply looked away? My contract only required me to present a forty-five minute presentation; it said nothing about spending time with the students. It would have been easy for me to dismiss the girl, hop on a plane and fly home. But sometimes life demands that we forget the contract and focus on our greater obligations to each other. I ignored the other kids around me and focused on *her*. All the while she spoke, I never let go of her eyes. Of course, she needed more help than I could give her. She needed counseling and support. But I gave her the one gift I was capable of giving: I did not turn away. I heard what every line of her face was screaming: LOOK AT ME. I looked and listened. *Please look at me.* I gave her that human connection that reminds us who we are and that we are not alone. I did what I could, and I know that she did not pull that trigger. She got help.

In an organization, behavior trickles down from the top. Your attitude toward passion, your own and that of others, will be reflected in the attitudes of others toward the passions of their colleagues. If you care, they'll care. If you dismiss, they'll dismiss. Try listening and caring about the passions of the people you work with and watch them transform before your eyes. It creates a workplace of trust, where people know their deepest loves will be respected and made safe. It gives them back their dignity. I call this the "Sherpa mentality." You are at the base of a mountain and your whole objective, your own passion, is not only to reach your own personal summit, but to make sure that you take the load off others so that they can reach their summits as well.

Caring on a Large Scale

One of the best examples of this kind of mentality was a company called Commercial Financial Services. Founded in Tulsa, Oklahoma, by Bill Bartmann, CFS was a collection agency that quickly became the standard for how corporations could and should treat their employees to create incredible productivity and incredible loyalty. Bartmann, a serial entrepreneur who had started many companies and also experienced failure and bankruptcy, built CFS into a billion-dollar giant by giving his employees an unbelievable package of perks and benefits.

This amazing company took 4,000 employees on trips to Disney World and other destinations. It bought cars for people whose cars had broken down. It had onsite health care and child care. But this is the thing that blows my mind: Bartmann would ask his employees what they had always wanted to do, and then he would make sure the company made it possible for them to do it! One employee said that he had always wanted to go and work with Mother

Teresa, so CFS paid for him to go on sabbatical and go to Calcutta to work with Mother Teresa helping the poor and sick. Unbelievable! As a result of all this largesse, CFS became incredibly profitable and had a turnover rate of something like four percent—in an industry where the typical turnover is twenty percent.

That's caring and passion writ large, and it transforms companies. It inspires people, makes them grateful and tells them they are important and special. CFS no longer exists due to an investment scandal, but that has nothing to do with the success of its focus on bringing out the best in its people. Shouldn't that be the mission of every CEO, pastor and professor? Doesn't a business benefit when it brings out the best in its people, even if that's not taught in an MBA program? Passion Principle:

> *Passion in an organization is about*
> *bringing out the best in everyone.*

The goal of the passion program in this book is to help professionals and executives build organizations in which passion is respected—where passions change from fragile china to tempered steel. Where people feel trust and safety, their passions become impossible to discourage. They become immune to criticism. They make an organization thrive.

The Practical Side of Passion

This chapter is largely for the practical professional who isn't about to toss aside his or her ten years of training and thirty years of wealth-building practice in order to go to Mongolia, live in a yurt and write free verse poetry. We all know that if you're making $250,000 a year in your dermatology practice, even if you feel stressed and bored with your work, you're not going to ignore your mortgage, run out on your responsibilities to your spouse and children, and join a commune. For one thing, the rewards of all that hard work are real and worthwhile: a nice house, a fancy car, financial security, the freedom (hopefully) to travel and take time off, and so on. You're not likely to surrender those, either.

One of the most important messages I give to my coaching clients and my speaking audiences is that you can increase your pleasure in the work you're doing today by weaving your passion into it. You don't have to make your passion your sole occupation; you can blend the two. Just like the guitar-loving orthodontist, you can work your passion into your daily working life without sacrificing the profession that's made you such a fantastic living.

The benefits you see in your individual career from pursuing your passion will depend on one factor above all: your commitment. The true development of passion is not a hobby, but a lifelong mission. Doing it right demands that you take your passion seriously and express it every day, even if it's in a small way. Passion is not an overnight fix, but something that needs to become a part of your career, just as integral as working with patients or clients and billing.

These are the practical benefits I've seen for the careers of the professionals I have worked with to bring their personal passions into their work:

Greater earnings. Professionals who are happier in their work really do earn more! I've seen this happen most often in this manner: a professional integrates his passion into his company and decides that he's underpaid. He decides to ask for a raise, forget about the consequences! He knows he's worth it. His superiors are so moved by his passion and charisma that they give him the raise. Something in him speaks to the hidden passion in them. The result is a higher income.

More productive time. Passion-powered professionals are simply more productive than those who plod along just going through the motions. Ennui sucks the life out of your work and makes you more likely to waste time. When you're in your "passion zone," you'll work long hours without being tired.

Better staff performance. Your office staff, assistants and other support personnel become inspired by your show of passion and your respect for their passion. As a consequence, they will work harder and smarter, further increasing your profitability and your client satisfaction.

More free time. Almost everyone I work with who embraces the idea of passion becomes a dedicated acolyte of the idea of free time. Some take time off to enjoy passions like fishing or travel, but others just realize they owe themselves more than endless work. Some of my coaching students end up restructuring their lives and taking months off per year to really savor life!

Greater recognition. One of the most obvious results of passion is the effect it has on other people. When you're in the center of your passion, it shines from you, and people respond to that. They draw energy from you, become inspired by you, and give greater weight to what you say and do. It's no accident that passionate professionals tend to receive greater recognition from their peers.

So in the end, even a practical approach to passion can bring you more money, more time, more satisfaction, happier employees and greater acclaim in your field. What's not to love?

The Passionate Entrepreneur

Entrepreneurs are, by definition, passionate. You have to be energized by passion for an idea to put your reputation, hard work and money on the line for years to bring something to life that no one else can see. But plenty of people have passion, and not all of them become entrepreneurs. So what's the difference between the office assistant with a great idea who never does anything about it and Jeff Bezos, who started Amazon.com?

I believe it's that entrepreneurs are often around people who enhance and encourage their passionate ideas in practical ways. Earlier I talked about the destructive effect that dismissal has on people who are talking about their passions, and that effect is cubed when you're talking about entrepreneurial thinking. Entrepreneurial brainstorms are extraordinarily fragile, and if the entrepreneur is discouraged in the beginning, he or she is likely to clam up and never think big again. But if the idea receives an enthusiastic reputation, entrepreneurs can become unstoppable. Environment is everything.

Obviously, there are entrepreneurs who need to be handled with care, because they can be loose cannons. Going into a business idea without proper planning, by the seat of your pants, can cost lot of money and waste a lot of time. But most entrepreneurs can profit from positive, passion-centered communication that encourages them to develop their concepts in a constructive, productive, aggressive way. When you find people who share your enthusiasm for ideas, it opens your mind and makes you more creative. I have a guy who works for me who is passion on two legs. When he comes to the office, his enthusiasm makes me be more creative and think of possibilities for coaching, books and programs I hadn't even thought of before. Passion Principle:

> *Passionate thinking is contagious.*

Where can you find this kind of support and communication? How about entrepreneurship conferences? Coaching? Online communities like StartupNation.com? This kind of limitless thinking is all around you; you just need to realize that if you're an entrepreneur, it's an asset and something you should be looking for as part of your business plan. When you hit obstacles in developing your great idea, nothing gets you back on track like passionate people who believe in what you're doing and can inspire new thinking.

The Passion of Teens

How do you capture an idea when you're in the shower? How do you capture an idea when you wake up in the middle of the night thinking, "Wow, that would change everything." You have a few seconds to capture inspiration before it's gone forever. People who are entrepreneurial in their spirit listen to their creative passion and capture those fleeting visions; people who are not dismiss their mental lightning bolts and go back to sleep.

So if you're an entrepreneur, how do you cultivate your passions and the ideas they produce? First, don't pre-qualify your ideas. I see this all the time: a woman will talk about an idea she had for a business, and immediately start talking herself out of it. Let the ideas flow! Until it's costing you money or you have investors looking for returns, what's to stop you from doing a thought experiment and taking your idea to its logical conclusion? Nothing. Entrepreneurial thinking becomes a habit when you spend time around people who elevate your thinking—who, when you propose an out-there idea, say, "Hey, that's interesting. What if you tried it this way?"

Teenagers are founts of this kind of free-form, fearless thinking. There's a simple reason for it: they haven't failed yet, so they don't know to be afraid of failure. If we put them in an environment where their passions receive encouragement, imagine the creative, visionary entrepreneurs we would produce! When it comes to our passions, we're all adolescents: nervous, afraid of criticism, worried about what others will think of what we say. But when we're put in an environment where we know that any idea we utter will be regarded with respect and enthusiasm, we can become genius machines.

I lead a passion-centered group of young people that meets on Sunday mornings in my office. I invite young people from our church, so rather than maybe having a Sunday school class, they come to my office for six weeks and we talk about being passion-centered and taking that passion into your adult life. "Don't wait until you are twenty-five or thirty years old," I tell them. "Go after it now." Passion is something innate to us all, something with a mysterious origin that we seem to be born with. It's spiritual. But the point is, by holding my group I am creating a space of trust, where young people feel safe expressing their passions and are encouraged to develop them while they are fearless.

If you really want passion, talk to a college student who was encouraged as a kid to have wild ideas and try them out. That's why the Internet revolution has been led by twentysomethings with big dreams and the willingness to believe, ignore convention, and above all, sacrifice. That's one of the most important aspects of passion for the entrepreneur. If you want to start something from scratch, you're going to have to be willing to sacrifice your time and your money, and to put your butt on the line with someone else's money. If you don't have the passion, sacrifice quickly turns into drudgery. But if you're passionate about your idea, nothing will keep you from making it a success. And that kind of never-say-die persistence is perhaps the signal feature of great entrepreneurs.

The Qualities of Passionate Entrepreneurs

Entrepreneurs built this country; they continue to build it. But are there qualities that passionate entrepreneurs have in common —qualities that you might see in yourself? I believe there are. Take a look at these and see if they look familiar:

- Enthusiasm—You have boundless positive energy for your ideas and are able to communicate it to other people and get them on board.

- Risk tolerance—You're not afraid to venture into unknown territory and put yourself on the line, fully aware that great things never happen without risk taking.

- Imagination—You think big and aren't limited by conventional wisdom. You tend to think around corners and come up with creative solutions.

- Belief—Once you know an idea is sound, your belief in it can't be shaken, no matter what anyone else says.

- Confidence—You have complete faith in your ability to bring your idea to fruition.

- Inspiration—You have a talent for getting other people energized by your idea and convincing them to put their rear ends on the line to make it a reality.

- Resilience—When circumstances knock you down, you always get back up.

A friend of mine, Scott Hagan, is the embodiment of all these qualities. Scott has more ideas than you can imagine, and a year or so ago, he came up with an idea that blew me away, and it's a wonderful example of passion playing out in the life of an entrepreneur. He came up with something called Mom's Prom. He reasoned that we had proms for our kids, so why not have proms for moms? Scott had shared this idea with some other people and they had said things like, "Oh, how nice." But he shared it with me and, recognizing the pure passion behind the idea, I told him it was a fantastic idea.

Because Scott could see my level of passion towards his idea, he came alive. We sat in my office and we broke it down, figured out what it would look like, how it would operate, and now Scott is in the process of bringing Mom's Prom to life as a business... and a passion. When somebody got excited about his idea, it validated the idea for Scott. My excitement unleashed more ideas from his phenomenal mind. What makes me sad is there are millions of people walking around right now who will never receive that kind of encouragement. Who knows? One of those people might have an idea that would truly change the world.

Do you have unexpressed passion that needs the right environment? Are you creating a passion-friendly environment in your workplace or home? Think about what you might be losing if you're not sharing your passion or encouraging others to share theirs. The rewards can be life-altering.

Now let's move to the next part of this journey: creating your plan to make your passion a part of your profession.

Passion Principles from this chapter:

> *Passion increases company productivity.*

> *Newly expressed passion is fragile.*

> *Passion in an organization is about bringing out the best in everyone.*

> *Passionate thinking is contagious.*

Part II:

Discovering Your Passion, Step by Step

Chapter Four

Put Your Passion In Writing

Passion very often makes the wisest men fools, and very often too inspires the greatest fools with wit.

—*François, Duc De La Rochefoucauld,*
French writer, moralist

Now that we've gotten the preliminaries out of the way, it's time to get down to the real work. Time for you to take a step back from your busy professional life and ask the question, "What am I missing?" Time to take a hard look at what seem like obligations in your life and discover that they are choices. Time to settle in with something to drink and let me walk you through the personal coaching regimen I use with all my coaching clients as well as some major companies.

The material in the coming chapters will rock your world, and I don't think it's an exaggeration to say that it will change your life. You'll discover the steps you need to follow to map out your passion and values, make a plan you can implement daily to bring you closer and closer to your passion, and understand how you can merge your passion and profession in a way that satisfies everyone in your life.

Let's start by putting your passion down on paper, shall we?

Your Passion List

Discovering and growing your passion is like any process: it begins roughly, with a lot of intense but unfocused effort, and graduates to more precise work that requires less energy but greater dedication. Your Passion List is where it all begins. As you feel your mind open to the idea that you can have more than you have now, the goal in this first step is to capture that feeling on paper (or computer) so it doesn't escape. As I've said and will say again, newly expressed passion is fragile. If you're a busy professional, you might feel a moment when your unrealized passion consumes you, but then the demands of work distract you from that feeling. If you don't capture it while it's hot... poof! It's gone with the wind.

So while you're still fired up from the first part of the book, sit down and write out your Passion List. This is an incredibly simple concept: just make a list of all the things you'd love to do if you had unlimited money, time and freedom. Don't edit yourself; this isn't about what makes sense or what you're "supposed" to be doing. This is about the voices that are screaming from deep in your soul: "Hey! I'm still here! You're not going to be happy without me, you know!" Turn off your inner editor (what I like to call your personal terrorist) and just write your list. Here's what I want you to write down:

1. Things you've always dreamed about doing.

2. Goals you haven't achieved yet but would still like to.

3. Things you would do even if you were never paid a dime.

4. Things you love. These can be activities, objects, emotions or even places.

Make a heading for each on your Passion List and go to town. Write down everything you can think of without pausing. Let yourself free associate. Go at it steadily for at least 30 minutes. Then if you find yourself blocked, take a walk. Walking is a wonderful stimulant for the thought process because while you're walking your mind drifts, which will break your block and bring new thoughts into your head. Go back and write those down.

Narrow It Down

Set aside your Passion List for 24 hours so you can clear your head. Go to work. Exercise. Follow your routine. Then when you have some quiet time, go back to your list and look at it. How many things did you list? Were you surprised by how much passion poured out of your pen or keyboard when you took the time to let it flow? That's what happens when we get in a place of passion: we express more than we ever thought we could.

Now is the time to become more analytical, to use your left brain more than your right. You need to begin narrowing down your passions. Living a passion-centered life means that instead of being all over the map and trying to do everything, you're going to choose one thing that sets your heart on fire and focus on it, exclusively. Remember Funnel Vision? That's passionate vision. One thing that exults and revitalizes you. No matter how great your list is, you can't do it all... at least, not now.

Looking over all the items on your Passion List, begin the process of narrowing them down to ten passions. Ten specific statements of things that you could make central to your life. It's a tough task, I know, but it's possible. The key is merging and blending different items on your list. For example, if one of your loves is animals, and one of your unfulfilled goals is to open a charity organization, then one possible passion might be to create a charity group that aids homeless and abandoned animals from the entertainment industry. See what I mean? Start working your list like a master carpenter: whittle it down. Your job in the next three days is to get that entire list broken down to ten passions, no more. If you only come up with seven or eight, that's fine. That means you're even more focused than most of my coaching students.

There Can Be Only One

OK, you have your list of passions. But you thought the narrowing process was over? Oh, you foolish mortal. Imagine me rubbing my hands together and cackling like a corny villain from a bad horror movie and telling you this:

Over the next 48 hours, you must narrow your passions to *five*.

Over the 48 hours after that, you've got to narrow them down to *three*.

And 48 hours after that, I expect you to be down to ONE passion that will become the new center of your life. *Mwahahaha!*

All kidding aside (and it's not easy for me to put all kidding aside; I'm a funny guy), this is a hard thing to ask of you. But like any demanding task, it's essential, and it's not really as difficult as it seems. You don't have to do it alone. Talk to your spouse, friends, pastor or co-workers. Think out loud about your passions. What's at least a little bit practical? What's neat but utterly impossible at this time? What's really not something you could spend the next twenty-five years doing? Is there a passion you're not ready to pursue now but could see yourself doing when you're 65? Then put that one away for a rainy day.

Ten to five isn't so bad. Five to three isn't a huge leap either; you're only cutting down by forty percent. But for most people, committing to one single passion is brutal. Well, here's a little tip for you: this isn't life and death. You're not signing mortgage papers or making a plea bargain. Choosing your one passion isn't irreversible. If you find out a few months down the line that the passion you thought you wanted to pursue just isn't right at this point in your life, you can go back and take a do-over, just like backyard baseball. But if you're anything like most of my students, you'll know what that one thing is that sends shivers up your spine.

If after a week you're still having a hard time getting down to a single passion, here are some questions that tend to help my students clear out the confusion:

- Look at your passion options. What stopped you from pursuing each one in the past?

- Do you feel obligated by someone else's expectations to pursue any of them?

- What passion do you pursue most when you have time that's completely free of anyone else's demands, expectations or judgment?

- What passion scares you the most?

- What passion can you best balance with the other aspects of your life that bring you satisfaction?

Eventually, you will winnow your list down to a single passion, something that blends the realistic practicality you may need, the sense of purpose that everyone needs in life, and the emotional satisfaction that serves as your fuel. Don't throw the other passions aside, however. Keep them, because you may want to refer to them later. Our lives are constantly changing, and what seemed like a passion that was impossible to pursue ten years before can seem inevitable when your life or your priorities change. Never discard or take your passions lightly. Tuck your list away for your future.

Why only one passion? Because when you are introducing something so radically transformative to your well-ordered life, you need to do it in manageable doses. You're going to be trying to handle your busy career, fulfill your obligations to family, friends and community AND take steps to follow and integrate your passion into your life. That's a lot of demands. Bringing more than one passion into the process simply isn't feasible. And anyway, passion is about focus, remember? You need to choose the passion that moves you and put your heart and soul behind it. If you have space in your life later, you can always chase down another passion.

Now your task is simple, but hard: *with your single passion in mind, write a single short phrase that describes what this passion signifies about what you were born to do or be.* Sound portentous? Not really. You're assigning meaning to your passion. What does it say about who you are and why you're on this earth? This could take a while, but it's worth the time. Think of this as your personal passion mission statement. This statement announces your passion to the universe and, more important, defines the kind of person you aspire to become by integrating your passion into your life. That's vitally important. You must know your destination if you're to make a successful journey. Here's an example: A guy I know is a very successful, busy journalist. But he also has a passion for music, particularly the blues, that consumes him. But for years it was unexpressed. He was just too busy. Finally, after years of long hours and stress, he decided to pursue his love of writing, singing and playing music. But before he did, he wrote his Passion Mission Statement:

"My work is my life, and my work has been about ideas and information, always edited by someone else and scrubbed clean of opinion and raw emotion. My music is all raw opinion and emotion, what I could never express to my audience before. Music is me—unamended and fully in the present."

Now, I don't expect your statement to be that eloquent; after all, the guy is a professional writer. It's also longer than I'd like, but that's OK. Try to stick to a single, short, simple idea, but if you need more words to say what you absolutely must say, then go for it. Take your time and make it perfect in your own eyes. Don't worry about what others think of it. Let them find their own passions. This is all yours, now and forever.

Your Core Values

Now that you've gone through all these arduous steps, I'll share something with you: passion isn't enough. Passion is the foundation for all the changes you will make, but it's not the only thing you'll need to make those changes lasting and positive. You must come to understand the duality between passion and *values*. In fact, that's a Passion Principle:

> *Passion without guiding values*
> *is a hobby or an obsession.*

Your passion is that thing you simply must do to serve the voice inside of you. That's wonderful, but it doesn't complete the transfiguration of that inner need to a productive external action. Values are what achieve that. You might know what your passion is, but your values tell you what your passion *means*. In bringing your passion into your profession, you are going to be forced to make choices. The choices may be small, like how to change the décor of your office to reflect your love of baseball. Or they may be dramatic, such as the decision to leave your real estate career to make wooden furniture as your grandfather taught you.

In any case, you'll arrive at forks in the road where choice becomes inevitable. When those choices come, your values are what will guide the choices you finally make. If you value material comfort over everything else, you'll make choices that will ensure your income doesn't drop. If you value spirituality most, you will make decisions that serve the edicts of your faith or allow you more time to explore your spiritual calling. Your values become the compass that guides your passion process. As I said, without values, your passion will become either a harmless hobby that doesn't change your life in the manner you hope for, or a dangerous obsession that's without meaning or purpose and can damage your career and your relationships.

Illuminating Questions

During one of my coaching sessions, I had one of my clients complete this exercise and write down his core values. It took a while and a lot of introspection, but in the end he became so inspired by this simple task that he took his list to a graphic artist and had it framed. For his birthday he gave that framed list to his family as a present. It now hangs in a special place in the family room— and in the hearts of his wife and four children.

A significant part of the passion process is self-discovery. You are flexing muscles that may not have seen action in years, maybe decades, and in doing so you're finding out things about yourself that you always knew but had forgotten... or willfully suppressed. Now the birds are coming home to roost, as they say, and the prospect can be uncomfortable. Are you who you hoped you would become? Are you proud of what have become your priorities? If the high-powered look into your innermost motivations and desires is difficult, that's all right. It's not supposed to be easy, just rewarding.

I say this because determining your most cherished personal values may be the most disarming part of this entire program. This is true because, like it or not, your values are your values. They may not be the same after you bring your passion to life in your work, but today, where you are is where you are. You may *wish* that you were a person whose highest values were charity, health and being nice to puppies, but you may not be that person... today. Setting down your core values is about being honest with yourself about what's most important to you right now. It may not be something that you're especially proud of. Like many professionals I work with, you may realize that you have spent years being most concerned about work and making money. And that is just fine. There are no wrong answers here; you need to admit who you are today and understand that as you open your eyes to your passion, you will become a different person—you will become more the person you aspire to be. Passion Principle:

> *The hardest part of finding your passion is admitting you're not who you wanted to become.*

The heart of discovering your core values is answering a series of what I call Illuminating Questions. These are ten questions about what matters to you most. But before we get to them, let's go over the ground rules for the Core Values part of our process.

Writing Your Core Values List:

- Limit interruptions. Find a quiet spot and make sure your cell phone is turned off.

- Answer the Illuminating Questions.

- Be brutally honest with yourself.

- Do not pre-qualify your responses. Just write. But keep in mind the way you live now and the limits you set for yourself.

- Try to do this exercise in one sitting.

- Don't worry about grammar; you can clean it up later.

- Complete the questions, then set the list aside. Come back in a few days and add to your list if needed.

- Show it to someone who knows you well and ask him or her to evaluate if your answers suit you. This is to ensure you are being honest with yourself.

- Revise as needed, then save your final list.

Now, the Illuminating Questions:

1. What would I be willing to die for?

2. What would I be willing to live for?

3. What do I believe in and why?

4. What would I never be willing to compromise?

5. What values that I see in others offend me?

6. What are the values that I want my children to adopt?

7. How do I adhere to my values when no one is watching?

8. What is my work ethic?

9. What do colleagues say I value?

10. What do my spouse and children say I value?

The Four "C Factors"

These are not easy questions. In fact, they may be the most challenging questions you have ever encountered. You may need considerable time to answer all the questions honestly and thoroughly. That's great. Take as much time as you need. Eventually you'll distill the answers down to simple, clear statements of your core values. But in the meantime, I want to offer you some help in confronting this personal challenge.

I know the questions are tough, because I answered them myself. There's nothing in this book that I haven't gone through personally, though when I was doing it, the steps had different names or no names at all. What I found, however, was that four ideas, each beginning with the letter "C," could help me get proper perspective on my values and the questions I had to answer. If you're having trouble with any of the questions, try reviewing the "C Factors" to help you get a handle on your own ethics, actions and beliefs. The "C Factors" are:

Character. What do you choose to do when you know you won't be subject to the judgment of others?

Consistency. Do your values change when your circumstances change, or are they consistent no matter what happens?

Conviction. Do you stick to your values even when the results they produce are not to your liking? Or do you abandon them when they are inconvenient?

Choice. The visible evidence of your values is in the choices you make each day. What kind of choices are you making?

When you have made it through this emotional and intellectual obstacle course, your reward will be greater self-knowledge and an unbreakable foundation for your pursuit of passion. So trust me when I say that even though it's hard, it's worth every bit of self-doubt and discomfort.

Core Values, Defined

We're almost there, but there's one more step to go. You have answers to the Illuminating Questions and some insight from the "C Factors." Now it's time to get thee to the distillery and refine that information down into core values. Everything we'll do in this book will consist of taking a large amount of unwieldy information and condensing it to short, clear, powerful statements of principle and action. That's what passion is all about: discovering the principle you want to live by, then taking action to make it happen!

Look at your answers to the ten questions and use that information to answer two more very direct questions:

What are the things you will always do, no matter what?

What are the things you will never do, no matter what?

Those are your core values. It's really that simple. People don't realize that their values can be broken down to such basic elements, but they can. The values that define us can be summarized as the things we will always do and the things we will never do under any circumstances. Examples of things good people will always do:

- I will always keep my children safe.

- I will always help people in my community who are in need.

- I will always travel and see the world.

And examples of things the same people will never do:

- I will never work for someone else.

- I will never cheat on my spouse.

- I will never use drugs.

Turn those statements into principles and you've got your core values, to which you can refer time and time again to keep you on the path toward a passion that fulfills who you are and helps you become the kind of person you always imagined you would be. As principles, the six examples above become:

- Protection of family
- Giving to others
- Travel and discovery
- Economic independence
- Fidelity
- Personal health and responsibility

You might come up with four or a dozen. It doesn't matter. Those principles are your core values, pressed out of all the previous questions and soul-searching like fine wine pressed out of rich grapes. Those values will become your guiding star for the development of your passion—the center to which your passion must always return. In fact, that's a Passion Principle:

> *Core values become the boundaries of your passion.*

That means that when you are caught up in the excitement of bringing your passion to life, your core values will always be there to remind you why you're doing it in the first place. If one of your core values is devotion to your family, and you find that following your passion is actually taking more time away from family than your career, you can check yourself. You can course correct, because you know that if you continue to put passion before family, you'll regret it. It will violate who you are.

That's why I say that passion without values can become obsession. If your passion is potent and compelling, you could become lost in it without personal moral and ethical rules to guide you. I've seen it happen; people trade one preoccupation for another, and an opportunity is squandered. With your core values revealed and in place, that won't happen to you.

Your Guiding Star

Congratulations! You've completed the first step in passion boot camp. You may exhale. Now, write or print your one passion that you're going to go after, and your core values statements. Do it big and bold. Post them on your office wall. Make them your screen saver. Keep them in sight and in mind. They will be your North Star, unwavering, as you continue this process.

Passion Principles from this chapter:

> *Passion without guiding values*
> *is a hobby or an obsession.*

> *The hardest part of finding your passion is*
> *admitting you're not who you wanted to become.*

> *Core values become the boundaries of your passion.*

Chapter Five

Create Passion-Centered Goals

Let me have wisdom, beauty, wisdom and passion,
Bread to the soul, rain when the summers parch.
Give me but these, and though the darkness close
Even the night will blossom as the rose.
> —*John Masefield, British poet, "On Growing Old"*

Goal setting is a common part of many self-improvement programs, but I think most of them go about it backwards. They ask people to start off by choosing goals, but what are those goals based on? If you don't possess the self-knowledge to understand why you want what you want, you can't make wise choices about your path for your future. That's why it's been so important to complete the steps in the last chapter, where you determined your passion and the core values that guide your life. I believe that only with those in place can you set goals that are truly meaningful to bringing your passion and your profession together in a way that enhances both.

Goal setting has always been a vital part of personal success, and when you're first discovering your passion, it's even more important. Passion can be overwhelming, and when you're thrilled by how it makes you feel, details can be, let's say, hard to come by. You might have a grand vision of your next career, but wake up one morning (after you've quit your job) saying, "Oops, I have no idea what to do next." Goals are like a personal lens that focuses and strengthens your energies so you're always applying them to achieve what you want. The trick is to set the right kind of goals and make them lofty enough so that you're forced to grow your talents and discipline.

No one ever built a passionate life from setting flabby goals. There's a reason that military boot camps practically kill cadets with physical drills and endurance training: soldiers don't survive war by knowing how to ballroom dance or shoot baskets. If you want to experience the joy and freedom of your passion, set goals that you've got to really climb to reach—and make them specific. A study in 1981 concluded that in ninety percent of laboratory and field tests on the effect of goal-setting, individuals showed better performance when the goals were challenging and specific than when they were general and easy.

Your right goals are like nobody else's. That's wonderful, because it means you're following a unique path. In setting your goals, I like to use the system known as the SMART method. It's used a lot in a corporate setting to create project goals, and it looks like this:

- Specific—The objective or goal is precisely defined

- Measurable—There's a defined method for measuring the goal, such as the money you make or the time you spend with your family

- Achievable—The goal must be challenging, but something you can do. If you set a goal of winning an Olympic gold medal in the 100 meters, you're probably setting yourself up for failure.

- Rewarding & Relevant—The goal must make sense for your passion, and there should be some kind of reward when you achieve it, such as greater health or more free time.

- Time—You need a deadline.

Here's proof of the power of goal setting. Researchers polled the Harvard graduating class of 1953 to find out how many of these intelligent, ambitious people had written down their goals and had a plan to make them reality. Surprisingly, only three percent had done it. But when the researchers followed up with the same group twenty years later, they found that the three percent of goal-setters were *richer than the other ninety-seven percent put together.* Goal setting is mighty powerful stuff.

Step One: Compare Your Paths

In this chapter, we're going to drive in the third of the four foundation supports for your passion: your passion goals. And we're not just talking about any old goals, but passion-driven, career-driven goals that serve every part of your life, from your need to earn a healthy living to your desire to express the deepest part of your being. My goal creation program has five distinct steps, and I'll walk you through each one in detail. When you've completed them, you should not only have your passion goals neatly laid out, but you will have a deeper understanding of what achieving your goals will bring you in your life and why you chose them in the first place.

Here's something extraordinary to ponder: before you opened this book you were walking a single path through your life. After you read the first words, that path split into two. Isn't that amazing? It happened because you became aware that your career path, which has dominated your life for years, was not your only path. You also have a "passion path," which you have now discovered. Your job is to bring the two paths together so you can follow both. That brings up our first Passion Principle for this chapter:

> *Do what you must do while focusing on what you love to do.*

You can and should continue to build your professional life, unless you decide for some reason to abandon it utterly, which most will not. But at the same time, you can bifurcate your energies and also give time and attention to what you love, your passion. Sometimes your career and passion will overlap; sometimes they won't. When they do, it's incredible. When they don't, so what? You can still experience the security and satisfaction of a thriving career while savoring the soul-deep glee and transcendence of doing what you have always wanted to do. The two can co-exist. That's what these parallel paths are all about.

In this step, I want you to sit down with a large piece of paper and a pencil. Now, graph the path your passion would lead you on if you were to follow it without any other considerations. Do this by first drawing a vertical line that represents the life you lead now. The space to the left of this line represents your creative, impulsive, passionate side. The space to the right represents your analytical, predictable, responsible, pay-the-bills side.

Next, plot the "passion points" that represent various milestones in your pursuit of your passion, remembering that in this exercise, you're not doing anything else. For example, if your passion is to play harmonica in a blues band, your first point might be "buy a great blues harmonica." Your next might be "Find a band to join," followed by "Cash in my stocks and go on tour for a year." I know it's a little extreme, but you get the point. The farther away from your current life the point is, the farther it should be from the center line, so "Going on tour with the Grateful Dead" might be pretty close to the edge of the page. Plot out six to eight points that might occur if you took your passion to its limit without worrying about the mortgage or professional education or what the neighbors think.

Next, you're going to plot out your career path, using the center line, your current life, as your starting point. Where will it lead you? Do the same thing as with your passion path: write down "career points" representing things like starting your own practice, becoming certified in a new specialty, making partner, or even getting a huge raise and buying a mansion. Again, the farther the point is from today, the farther the point from the center line. Eventually, you should end up with something that looks like this:

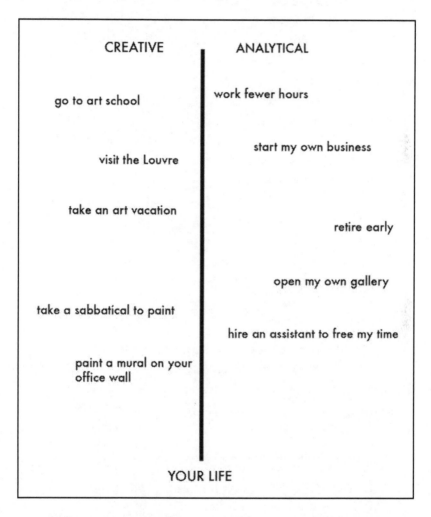

Now connect the dots and compare the two paths. How close are they? Do they diverge completely? Do they get close at any point? The farther they are apart, the more work you have to do to bring your passion and profession together. Your goal is to bring passion and career together along the center line.

Step Two: Integration

Now that you know how far apart your ideal passion-centered life and your ideal profession-centered life are, you need to figure out how to start merging them. To do that, you need to know how your passion can create your position. What I mean by that is, how can your passion cause your career to evolve?

Take a look at your working life as it is today. Write down every aspect of your typical day, including the hours you work, what you do at lunch, what you talk about with patients or clients, and so on. Then brainstorm ways that your passion could be integrated into that working life. Could you set aside more time off for your passion? Change your work environment? Get your practice involved in a charity related to your passion? There are always ways. Make a list, without letting your mind edit your items, of any ways, both simple and radical, that your passion could work into your career.

Step Three: Your Perfect Day

This is the step most of my coaching clients have the most fun with. Imagine your absolutely perfect workday. Forget about your normal work routine, the clients or patients you see, the paperwork you must do, the cases or study you have to work on. Instead, map out your ideal day, with only two rules:

You must be at the place you work now.

You must engage in work that makes you money.

The best way to do this is to map out a 9:00 to 5:00 schedule and fill in activities at one-hour increments. This is a very enlightening exercise, because it really makes you stop and think about the aspects of your work that you really enjoy. I find that many people I work with are surprised, because the parts of their work that they enjoy are often the ones they do the least. This might be the "familiarity breeds contempt" effect. For example, dentists frequently say they most enjoy talking with patients about their lives, while the aspect of their work they like the least, unsurprisingly, is dealing with insurance companies.

What does your perfect day look like? How do you earn your income? Are you doing any of these things today in your work? In the end, you should develop enough insight into the changes you must make to incorporate your passion into your profession. When you've taken some time to consider the meaning of your "perfect day" schedule, fill in the following blank:

I would enjoy my work 100% more if I just _____.

Remember, changes that radically increase your enjoyment of your work won't always be dramatic. Does your work allow you to potentially work at home? Making that move could facilitate your passion. There may be many ways to bring your passion into your professional life. Be creative. Ask other people for their suggestions.

Step Four: Short-Term Goals

At this stage you should have a clearer idea of several things: how far apart your current reality and ideal reality are, what aspects of your passion you could integrate into your profession, and what your perfect day would look like. The purpose of those exercises is simple: you can't set solid goals until you know what you're trying to achieve. So now the time has come to set some goals.

Keeping the SMART strategy in mind, on your computer or a sheet of paper, write out ten "passion-centered goals" you would like to achieve in the next three months. They should be goals that will bring you a little bit closer to making your job the perfect job, thereby making each day perfect. These goals can and should be process-oriented; that is, they can be the steps in bringing your passion into your work, rather than the passion itself. In other words, if your passion is to integrate your yoga practice into your work as a realtor, one of your goals might be to create a yoga space in your office. You could even make each step involved in creating this space a goal unto itself. See where I'm going with this?

Two pieces of advice. First, once you have your list, put it someplace you can see it every day. This creates a visual reminder of what you're trying to achieve, in essence making your goal list your to-do list. Second, make your three-months goals achievable. There will be a time for grand goals, but this is not it. It's important to your pursuit of passion to set goals that you can reach with reasonable effort. This creates positive feedback energy that will encourage you and motivate you. To quote a Passion Principle:

> *Start with the ridiculous to reach the impossible, not the impossible to end up with the ridiculous.*

Change is not instantaneous. Making the front end of your goal setting easily reachable may have you doing some things that seem insignificant or, as I say, ridiculous. To go back to the previous example, one goal in creating your yoga space might be finding a perfect pillow, which could seem silly if you never spend any time in a home furnishings store. But it's part of your journey that serves your larger goal, so you must honor it.

Going the other way, setting huge goals to achieve ends that are simply not realistic is a recipe for failure. Going back to the blues band example, if you're a 55-year-old stockbroker with a wife, four kids and a big mortgage, no matter how much you love the blues, it's just not in the cards that you'll quit your job and leave to go on a world tour with Taj Mahal and his band. Could you do it? In theory, I suppose. In the real world, no.

Step Five: Long-Term Goals

Now it's time for the big goals, the life-transforming steps that will happen over a greater period of time but will bring greater joy to your life than you ever thought possible. You're going to write out your long-term goals for one year, three years and five years, keeping your passion at the center.

This is like making a map for a great journey. Each goal from year to year is sequential and cumulative, so if you set a goal for Year One, your Year Three goal needs to reflect that Year One goal's achievement. These goals should also track a journey, but this is a journey of greater change. Over one to five years, you can make immense changes in your professional life, and your long-term goals should reflect those changes. They should track your move from passion and profession being on completely opposite sides of that center line to sharing much of that line.

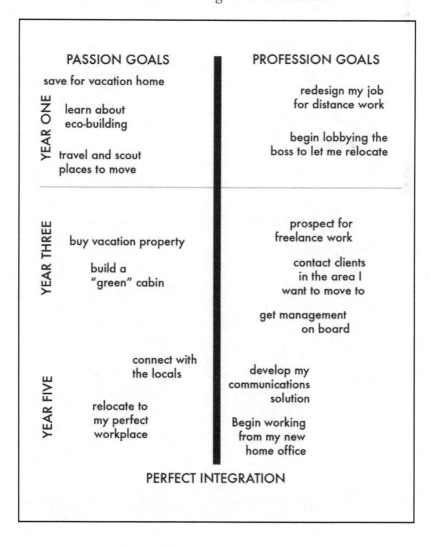

PASSION GOALS

YEAR ONE

save for vacation home

learn about eco-building

travel and scout places to move

PROFESSION GOALS

redesign my job for distance work

begin lobbying the boss to let me relocate

YEAR THREE

buy vacation property

build a "green" cabin

prospect for freelance work

contact clients in the area I want to move to

get management on board

YEAR FIVE

connect with the locals

relocate to my perfect workplace

develop my communications solution

Begin working from my new home office

PERFECT INTEGRATION

As you write these goals, express them as "I will" statements, not "I want to" statements. These are not optional actions you're talking about; they're central to your happiness and wholeness as a human being. Your language as you talk about your goals will determine your level of determination to reach them; that in turn will determine your success. Bold statements make us bold. State your goals confidently to the universe and you bring them closer to realization.

Don't Give Up, Take Up

One final word before we move on from this short but important chapter. Bringing your passion into your profession is not about what you *stop* doing, but what you *begin* doing. When I talk with professionals about making these broad changes, one of the first questions they ask is "What do I have to give up?" My answer: nothing you don't want to give up.

Following your passion is about doing new things that make a difference in how you feel, or about doing old things in a new and better way. You may stop activities that feel unsatisfactory to you, but that will come about organically, because you find ways to spend your time that better serve your passion. Your passion should not compel you to quit your job (unless that's absolutely what's right for you); it should transform your work to make you do it better. Take up actions that bring your passion alive within the boundaries of your profession, and that will make all the difference. Let's turn this into a Passion Principle:

> *It is not what you stop doing but what you start doing that makes all the difference.*

With your goals in mind, let's move on and take a look at the last support in the foundation of the monumental changes you're on the verge of making: determining your vision for your future.

Passion Principles from this chapter:

> *Do what you must do while focusing on what you love to do.*

> *Start with the ridiculous to reach the impossible, not the impossible to end up with the ridiculous.*

> *It is not what you stop doing but what you start doing that makes all the difference.*

Chapter Six

Your Vision

There is in most passions a shrinking away from ourselves. The passionate pursuer has all the earmarks of a fugitive.
—*Eric Hoffer, U.S. philosopher*
The Passionate State of Mind

One of the most vital points about passion is this: it doesn't happen by accident. This section of the book—all these steps I'm slowly walking you through—reflect that. When you're planning to make a major change in how you live your life, from incorporating your passion into your work to changing your career completely, you need to know what you're doing before you get started, or disaster is inevitable.

In this chapter, we're going to dig our final hole and cement the final foundation support for your passion: vision. We're going to take the single passion, values and goals that you've distilled in the previous two chapters and turn them into a cogent, cohesive vision for your professional life—a guiding star, if you will. Right now you have a lot of raw information that may be compelling, but it isn't a plan. It's like being a mechanic in a garage: you might have a fuel injector, an alternator and some cylinder heads, but they're not an engine until you put them together in the right way. I'm going to show you in this chapter how to extract a compelling vision for your future from all that raw data, and that vision is going to carry you into a thrilling tomorrow. Ready?

Imagine It, Then Create It

Where you have no vision for how you want your life to progress, your dreams will fail. Vision is like the coach, and passion is the team of horses. You must have both. A vision without passion is motionless, but a passion without vision is a fantasy. You can only become the person you know deep inside that you want to become when you embrace a clear vision for what tomorrow will look like.

Here's the example I like to give my audiences. Imagine you're an architect. If you are an architect by profession, play along and imagine your typical workday. OK? Before you can draw a single line of the plan for that grand new building you've been commissioned to design, it has to exist in your mind. You have to have a vision of what the building will look like, down to the last brick. You don't have to know where the wiring and ducts will go, but you must have that detailed, comprehensive vision to guide your hand. Well, you're the architect of your life, and before you can take action to pursue your passion and reach your goals, you need a clear vision of what your life will look like a few years from now.

My point is, to create it you have to imagine it first. It's true: every great invention, work of art, book, building and even institutions like our Constitution began as ideas in the imagination of a person. That person took that idea, fleshed it out in his or her mind, then took action to make the idea tangible. That's a kind of magic. From nothing more than an idea we've gotten the Internet, *Hamlet*, and modern jurisprudence. That's the power of a vision made manifest. Once you can imagine your life being different, the only thing stopping you is you.

The Law of Courage

What's often stopping people from taking that leap into passion is their own apprehension about taking a misstep. "What if I do something drastic to pursue my passion and it turns out to be the wrong thing?" they ask me. My response is always the same: if what you're doing is in service of your true passion, that thing you were meant to do or person you were meant to be, there is no such thing as wrong. You can't make a mistake. Anything you do will be right, even if in the short term it feels wrong.

However, let's be honest. It does take courage to turn your back on what you know. Inertia is a powerful thing. A body at rest tends to stay at rest. It becomes very easy to stick with what you've been doing because it's familiar. You can delude yourself into thinking, "One day it will change." I'm here to tell you that it won't. Not unless you take courageous action. And that's where what my co-author Tim Vandehey calls the Law of Courage comes into play.

The Law of Courage is incredibly simple and incredibly powerful. It states that whenever you take courageous action in the face of life's doubts, you cannot go wrong. You will always improve yourself and your life. Every time. When you have a choice between taking the easy way out that doesn't make you nervous, or the hard way out that tests your courage, take the hard way. Make the courageous choice. You'll be amazed at the power one courageous act has to transform you. Courage tends to cascade, meaning that one act can lead to multiple good things coming your way, feeding off each other.

So as we move ahead with this process and you start to think about your vision, be courageous with it. Think bold and big. Dare to challenge yourself and push the envelope. Punch a hole in the sky. Scare the daylights out of yourself, then do it anyway. Nothing, and I mean nothing, is more empowering. Obey the Law.

Your Career Vision Statement

The first thing you're going to do is craft a "vision statement" for your career. This vision statement will define what your career will be like one year from now, after you have successfully integrated your deepest passion into your work. This is a best-case scenario based on your realistic goals, but also on your values and your desire to get the greatest joy and satisfaction from your working life. So while you shouldn't do a pie-in-the-sky vision, you shouldn't sell yourself short, either. Make your vision statement realistic, but ambitious and aggressive.

Your vision statement can be as long or short as you like, as basic or as detailed. There are no wrong answers here. Your job is to paint a verbal picture of the working life you want to have twelve months from today. How do you want to be spending your time? How do you want to *feel* at the beginning and end of the day? How will you get there from where you are now?

Sit down and give this some time. Take at least an hour to go over your passion, values and goals.

Nine Tips for Writing Your Vision Statement

1. **Base it on your passions, not your current position or your ability to make money.** Your vision should center on your passion. You already know how to make a buck at what you do. Don't worry about the implications of working your passion into your career. Just figure out what you will do and your method, and let the chips fall where they may.

2. **Your vision must be fueled by faith in something, not fear of something.** You won't make bold decisions if you make them out of fear of losing money, embarrassing yourself or even growing old without knowing what it feels like to live passionately. You'll make safe, uninspiring decisions that you won't follow through on. Instead, have faith in the truth of your passion and the power of that passion to transform your life.

3. **Know what you are passionate about, not simply proficient at.** You may not be great at whatever your passion is right away. If you've always wanted to play the violin but have never taken a lesson, you're going to stink at first. That's all right. Don't go easy on yourself by building your vision around something you're good at for its own sake. If you're passionate about it and great at it, that's wonderful. But passion is more important than skill level.

4. **Your gifts, talents and abilities might have nothing to do with your passion.** You might be a great doctor with a keen analytical mind. But that may have zero intersection with your passion for old radio shows. Your passion doesn't have to feed off of your natural gifts, though it can. It should stand on its own, and if it has nothing to do with your greatest area of talent, so what? Don't be fooled into thinking what you're gifted at or trained in is your passion.

5. **Start by writing down conceptual "big ideas" for how you can change your professional life. Then work down to the details. Starting with the minutiae will bog you down.** Think big and have fun at first imagining what your career could be like. Don't let practical considerations slow your creativity. There's plenty of time for the nuts and bolts. Just make sure that your vision is in line with your realistic goals.

6. **Once you have the conceptual down, list the practical.** How do you see the details of your professional life—where you live, how much you make, how long you work—changing? What steps must you take to bring your passion into your career?

7. **Consider the internal changes you will need to make in your professional life—new personnel, cutting costs, getting new clients, etc.—to achieve your vision.** Make a new business plan for yourself, mapping out all the professional steps you'll need to take.

8. **Write down your goals from Chapter 6 as a reference point.**

9. **With your goals, conceptual ideas and practical steps in mind, write your vision statement.** This is a single sentence that states where you will be, when you will be there and what kind of working life you will be living when you have fully integrated your passion into your nine-to-five life. Make your statement brief but vivid and declarative ("I will" versus "I may").

Some sample vision statements:

- *I will scale back my corporate law practice to spend more time doing pro bono work for groups that fight hunger in Africa.*

- *I will leave my corner office and work at home three days per week, giving me more time for my children and my garden.*

- *I will use my financial planning experience to write a book and go on the speaking circuit instead of working 60-hour weeks for my clients.*

Note that the statements are descriptive but do not go into painful detail. That's deliberate. You want to inspire yourself with a broad vision, not depress yourself with a laundry list of all the steps you have to take to bring that vision into existence. We'll get into the details later in this chapter, using the conceptual and practical information you wrote. For now, bask in the pleasure of having a clear vision on paper.

Making Big Changes

Ah, lists. If only life were so easy as making lists. If introducing tectonic changes into our lives was only a matter of jotting down bullet points on our laptops, we would all be wealthy, slender and successful... just like me. But seriously, lists are great, but only a starting point. The exercises in this section of the book have two purposes: one, to help you develop organizational tools for making your passion a reality, and two, to make you think about who you are, what you're doing and what you want. The second purpose is actually more valuable, because you can write a list long enough to reach the moon, and nothing will happen unless you also change your *attitude*.

I'm a firm believer that very few people enact large-scale changes to their lives unless they are in crisis. Most of the time, we rationalize our unhappiness or depression and keep doing what we're doing; a body in motion tends to stay in motion. That's a Passion Principle, also known as Gary's Law of Passion Inertia:

> *You will not pursue your passion until you deliberately initiate your own crisis.*

The word "crisis" has many negative connotations, but in this context I think it's only positive. The word *crisis* stems from the Latin word *krisis*, meaning "decision," and one of its dictionary meanings is "an unstable or crucial time or state of affairs in which a decisive change is impending." A crisis is a time of opportunity that is usually so emotionally destabilizing that it forces us to examine our attitudes and actions—to take the "look in the mirror" that can be so difficult—and see clearly how we're sabotaging ourselves. Often, the times in our lives that are the most emotionally painful can be the most rewarding and positive in the long term, because only during such times do we become self-aware enough to truly redirect our lives.

In part, the passion process is about invoking such a crisis period in your own life, related to your profession. By having you make all these lists and asking all these tough questions, I'm hoping to guide you into a place of introspection, where you'll take an honest appraisal of where you are and why you're not happy. Then, when you reach that point of openness, you can begin to make the mental and emotional changes that will allow you to put these lists to work and make your vision a reality.

These are the emotional and mental territories that will need some transformation if you are to successfully materialize your vision:

- **Belief**—You must believe that you can and will follow your passion no matter what opposition appears. Remember, passion will always be tested by opposition. Your pursuit of your passion cannot be an "I sort of want to do this" enterprise, or you will fail. You must believe with every bone in your body that you can and will make it happen.

- **Gratitude**—Be grateful for the successes you achieve along the way. The road will not always be smooth, and if you've had a great deal of success in your career, you might have a tendency to be overconfident. Be grateful for the small victories you achieve and forgive yourself when you have setbacks.

- **Humility**—Humility goes along with gratitude. You may have aced medical school or passed the bar on the first try, but that means nothing when it comes to the heavy lifting of changing your life. Don't assume you're unconquerable, because you're not. Give yourself permission to make mistakes and have setbacks. You will experience both, and only with some humility will you forgive yourself and others and bounce back.

- **Resiliency**—You will experience resistance from others when you begin to chase your passion. Some people will just question and cast doubt in your mind; others will openly criticize you, scorn what you're doing and insult your professionalism. Develop the thick skin that comes from knowing you're doing what's right for you, and that the criticism comes from people's lack of understanding, not from anything you are doing wrong.

- **Sacrifice**—You will give things up when you pursue your passion. Get used to it. You must accept the fact that you will be asked to give up your *lust* for life so you can embrace your *love* of life. That means you may end up giving up some of your more shallow pleasures in order to embrace your life's meaning. Be ready to surrender things that don't matter to embrace what does.

- **Acceptance**—Becoming a passion-centered professional means you must accept the passions of others, even if you disagree with them. Once you're part of the passion club, you accept the responsibility of encouraging other people to discover and express their passions. This is serious business. You have the power to promote or kill the passions of others.

What Do You Expect?

Setting goals is a wonderful thing, but how do you know when you've reached them? How do you know when you've fully incorporated your passion into your profession? When you are making monumental changes in your life, it's important to have benchmarks to gauge your progress. You must know when you've reached your goals in order to keep yourself motivated. It's also essential to know when you can celebrate what you have achieved, because this is a huge deal and you need to reward yourself when you reach a milestone.

So write down the benefits you think you will see as you come into your passion. This is guesswork, true, but who is in a better place to predict than you? Make a list of the benchmarks you expect to reach as your passion comes to fruition. You can get into specific numbers, such as an increase in revenue, if you want to, but it's not required.

Some examples of the telltale benefits you might experience when your passion and working life are aligned:

- **Greater productivity.** Passion motivates us to go beyond what is expected. When you work in passion, it's not work. You'll make better use of your time and your ideas.

- **Greater profitability.** Passion will usually improve your bottom line. People love to invest in those who bring real passion to what they do, and greater productivity leads to greater profits.

Deeper relationships. People are inspired by those who live their
passion. You will likely find that your passion inspires others
and attracts those who have the same desire to live in passion
that you have.

• **Greater pleasure.** If you're doing what you were born to do,
how can you ever be bored or cynical?

I suggest combining your expectations with a timeline, so that
you can write something like, "By September, I expect to have re-
duced the hours I spend in the office by twenty-five percent." That's
an example of getting into quantifiable information, which is OK.
The more precise your benchmarks can be, the better. But don't ob-
sess about earning more or working less, or you'll focus on the benchmark and not the passion. If you enjoy your work more and work
the same number of hours, that's success. The idea is to make your
life richer and more meaningful, not to check off a series of milestones like you're going down your shopping list. Passion Principle:

> *Passion is about the quality of your life,*
> *not the quantity of your successes.*

The most important benchmark of this journey is how you
feel. It's good to have milestones to strive for, but they shouldn't
take the place of the joy and satisfaction you experience from
simply having the courage to approach your passion in the spirit of
change and to begin letting this long-buried side of yourself loose.
That's the greatest reward of this entire process—becoming who
you were born to be.

Getting Specific and Taking Action

This has been a great deal of preparatory work, but now it's
time to get down to business. With all this self-knowledge, goal awareness and vision in your hip pocket, you're going to begin taking small

steps to bring your passion into your professional life right now. Not next week. Now. Tomorrow morning.

This is where you will finish the move from the abstract to the concrete. We've been moving along that continuum for a while, but now we get specific. You're going to map out practical actions that will get you started on your passion journey. This can be scary, because up to now we've been talking about ideas that are pretty broad and nebulous, things you can do without having anything at stake. That time is over. Time for the rubber to meet the road.

Go back to your computer or pad of paper and begin writing down things you can do to bring your passion into your professional life right now. Here are some of the examples I have seen from my students:

- Keep something in your office or workplace that reminds you of your passion. It doesn't have to be as extreme as my guitar-loving dentist, but do something to change your environment.

- Start associating with colleagues who have a passion for life. Tell them about your passion and swap stories.

- Schedule a once-per-week "passion power lunch." Invite someone to lunch for the purpose of finding out what his or her passion is.

- If you want to energize the culture of your work environment, begin discovering the passions of your co-workers. People come alive when you ask them what they live for.

- Set aside thirty minutes every day at lunchtime to do something related to your passion.

- Stop working overtime and start ending the day at a predictable time, the first step toward taking greater control of your time.

- Set aside one day a week to take classes or instruction related to your passion at a local community college or your city's education program.

Your own examples will of course be unique to your situation, but you get the idea. Try to map out at least five specific things you can do in the next few days to begin bringing your passion into the front of your thinking as you are working. They don't have to be huge in impact; they just have to be things you will do consistently.

Selecting your single passion, determining your core values, setting your goals, cultivating self-knowledge about what's really important to you—they have all been leading to this place. You've made a vast amount of progress just in your thinking. If you're like most of the people I speak to, you have moved from a "My passion is stupid" mindset, through stages of self-doubt and denial, to a place where a passion-centered professional life seems not only possible but probable. That's a gigantic shift in your thinking, and it was always possible. You've moved from a vision that exists only in your mind to one that will begin to take shape in your physical experience.

The Five Percent

I want to leave you with one more thought before we move ahead to your Passion Plan, in which you will map out every step in the process of bringing your passion alive in your work. That thought is this: do not be afraid to consider the idea of leaving your current work behind and chasing your passion full-time.

I'll be honest with you: this sort of thing does not happen very often. As appealing as it sounds when you're shooting the breeze over a cup of latte, it's not an easy thing to do. The idea of dumping a twenty-year health care or financial career to raise sled dogs or do hubcap sculpture simply isn't practical or desirable for ninety-five percent of professionals. It may not be for you. You have bills. You have kids who want to attend college. You have obligations. And most important, *you still like what you do.* That's an essential distinction to make. I work with many, many individuals who still enjoy being doctors, corporate executives or engineers. They just don't like *how* they do their work. The time required, the conditions or the people make them miserable, but the work itself is enjoyable. They don't want to jettison their life's work; they want to rediscover what they loved about it in the first place by dumping all that extra garbage that robs their work of its pleasure.

However, you might be one of that five percent who are ready to quit and make a radical jump into a new career. In my experience, professionals who will do this are likely to have at least one of these factors:

- They have made their money and can afford to "retire" from their career.

- They don't have kids depending on them.

- They got into their line of work because of family expectations or because they wanted to make money, not because they loved it.

If you fall into any one of those groups, you're more likely to be ready to say, "Enough! I'm moving and not leaving a forwarding address." Even if you don't, you may be ready to leave it all behind. If you are, don't be discouraged by the information that's aimed at professionals who still want to do what they're doing and integrate their passions. The same steps in this process apply to you, too. In fact, if you're one of that motivated five percent, you're one of the blessed. You have the means and the motive to make a fresh start. Take the opportunity.

Explore how you feel about the idea of leaving it all behind, whether that means starting your own business or doing something else entirely. Ask yourself if that's a dream of yours. It may not be. Give it some time and listen to what you really want. There are no wrong answers, only truths we fail to tell ourselves.

Passion Principles from this chapter:

> *You will not pursue your passion until you deliberately initiate your own crisis.*

> *Passion is about the quality of your life, not the quantity of your successes.*

Chapter Seven

Make Your Passion Plan

If I were to wish for anything, I should not wish for wealth and power, but for the passionate sense of the potential, for the eye which, ever young and ardent, sees the possible. Pleasure disappoints, possibility never. And what wine is so sparkling, what so fragrant, what so intoxicating, as possibility!

—*Soren Kierkegaard, Danish philosopher*

All right, you've got your paints. You've got your canvas. You've got your easel and one of those goofy-looking palettes with a hole in it for your thumb. Now you're ready to make like Vincent Van Gogh and paint a thrilling new picture for your professional life… minus the ear amputation part. That picture is your 21-Day Passion Plan.

Incidentally, Van Gogh is a perfect example of how passion without values to guide it can become obsession. The Dutch master painted many of his greatest works during the last few years of his life, when he was unquestionably mentally ill, yet it's hard to see from his writings or biographies how the work gave him much joy. His passion and his great talent weren't matched by a values system and purpose that could guide and shape them. We're going to avoid all that by creating a plan to guide the beginnings of your journey toward becoming a passion-centered professional.

Why 21 Days?

Why not? Seriously, 21 days is a perfect length of time. It's long enough for some substantial changes to start taking place, but not quite a month. There's a reason for avoiding a month-long calendar: planning by the month makes it too easy for you to fall into patterns, and this is about creating new patterns.

There are many reasons for creating a written plan as you move toward developing your passion in your professional life. The most important is also the simplest: you're about to embark on a major life change, and you're going to lose focus, become discouraged and foul up. It's inevitable. But when you do, and you lose track of what you're doing and the destination you're bound for, your Passion Plan gets you back on track. It jogs your memory and brings you back to the present, because according to the plan there are things you need to be doing today, right now, so you'd better get with it. The plan is an insurance policy, breadcrumbs to keep you from losing your way.

It's also a hedge against doubt from others. Let me tell you right now, your pursuit of your passion is not going to thrill everyone in your office or practice. You're going to step on some toes. Your boss may be irritated and convinced you're planning to quit. Some colleagues might think you're a flake, while others will consider you conceited. How you deal with such people is up to you, but the last thing you want is for them to derail you from your pursuit. Your plan keeps you focused on the goals that will lead you to your passion.

Creating Your 21-Day Plan

The rules for the 21-Day Passion Plan:

1. Write out your complete plan in a form you can keep with you at all times. That could mean doing it on your home PC and copying it onto your computer at work, putting it on your PDA, or writing it in your Passion Journal (more on the journal later in this

chapter). I suggest you always have a second copy of your plan somewhere safe, just in case.

2. Start your 21-Day Passion Plan and keep notes on your progress for each of the 21 days.

3. At Day 21, assess the progress you've made toward your passion-based goals.

4. Revise your plan accordingly and start a new 21-Day Passion Plan. You should always be in the middle of a plan.

5. Do the best you can. You will make progress in some areas and fall backward in others. That's normal. You can adjust in your next 21 days.

OK, let's start putting the plan together. Choose whatever medium you like to write it out, and include each of the following components:

1. Your vision statement.

Write down the vision statement you developed in Chapter 7. It should encompass your passion, your core values, your professional goal, and how you see yourself living in the future. This is the guiding law, the Constitution, of your plan.

2. Your core values.

List all your core values from Chapter 5. They are reminders of your character and the path you wish to walk on the way to your passion.

3. Your goal(s) for the end of the 21 days.

Where do you want to be at the end of these three weeks? In what ways do you want to be closer to passion/profession alignment? List your goals for this limited period, remembering to keep them attainable. Remember, start with the ridiculous and progress to the impossible; the other way around doesn't work.

You will probably not reach all these goals every 21 days. That's OK. Remember, we're thinking long-term, not short-term. Progress is what matters. Forward motion is the stuff of hope.

4. The specific changes you will make in 21 days.

This is a big one. You have a goal or goals in mind; now you need to write down the changes you want to make in your personal and professional life in the next 21 days to help you reach those goals. Categorize these changes using a simple color-coded system:

RED CHANGES—Major changes that could alter the course of your professional life or job. These might include giving your notice, moving to a new residence, or altering a personal relationship.

YELLOW CHANGES—Moderate changes such as going back to school, taking up a new hobby, or disposing of some personal possessions.

GREEN CHANGES—Small changes like bringing a reminder of your passion to work, taking a new route to the office, or wearing different attire.

5. Your new daily schedule.

Part of pursuing your passion is doing things differently during your workday—making time for small activities that relate to your passion, or setting aside a few minutes each day to complete some tasks toward the launch of your own business. It could also be as simple as setting aside ten minutes a day for silent meditation. It all depends on your vision and goals.

With those in mind, map out your normal workday, and on that graph, write in the things you will do during that time. Nothing is too small; if part of your passion is going out of your way to smell the flowers in the lobby, write it down! Keep in mind that you will not be able to get to all these things every day; we all know that life intrudes, crises arise and %$#@ happens. But with this map, you'll achieve a lot.

6. Your new habits.

We are our habits, so your success in your move toward your passion will be defined by the habits you acquire and the habits you shed during your pursuit. Looking at your goals and where you are today, start writing about habits:

- New habits that serve your passion that you want to develop.

- Bad habits that don't serve your passion that you want to lose.

- The steps you will take to develop your new habits—reminders, visual cues, asking people to pester you, whatever.

- The steps you will take to shed bad habits—throwing away cigarettes, changing grocery shopping patterns, whatever it takes.

Also, write down the ways you will create "holes in your life," periods of empty space and time where new habits can suggest themselves and take root. If you're a busy professional, such "holes" are probably rare or nonexistent. But that's your choice, and you can change it. Eliminating negative habits or pursuits from your life— things that do not serve your passion—will create those empty spaces and allow new, passion-centered people, events and ideas to fill them.

7. The ways you will take your passion to work.

List all the ways you will begin incorporating your passion into your professional life. These steps can range from the ridiculous to the sublime, the innocuous to the outrageous. The idea is to build, slowly, a professional environment for yourself where virtually everything you see, hear and experience is either related to or reminds you of your passion and your vision.

List the ways you might take your passion to work, such as:

- Playing certain kinds of music in the office.

- Decorating your office or cubicle a certain way.

- Reading certain books during break times.

- Engaging your colleagues about their passions.

- Arranging after-work events for you and your colleagues that revolve around your passion.

- Printing your own custom business cards that state your passion and possibly a new, passion-centered job title.

- Be creative! Have fun with this.

8. Tricks to remind you of your passion and goals.

Days get busy and the mind wanders. It's easy to forget that during each day in your 21-Day Passion Plan, you have goals to meet and a schedule to keep. Not to worry. I've anticipated that. Part of your plan involves coming up with a series of tricks and memory triggers to remind yourself through the day to keep moving in the direction of your passion and your vision. These are a few ideas; you're welcome to write down and use your own, so long as they work:

- Sticky notes all over your workspace with pithy reminders on them.

- E-mail reminders from scheduling software.

- Watch alarms.

- Reminders written to yourself in your day planner.

- Mental triggers—"Every time I smell a new pot of coffee in the break room, I'm going to make another phone call related to my new company."

- E-mails or calls from friends conscripted to bug you.

Of course, I find the best reminder is the least discreet: your Passion Plan printed out extra-large and stuck on the wall opposite your desk, where you can't help but see it. If you don't have a great deal of privacy at work, this may not work for you. But if you're fortunate enough to have your own office, this is a great way to constantly jog your memory…and maybe instill a little touch of guilt. I'll take guilt. I'm not proud.

9. People who could be your Accountability Coaches.

We all need someone to hold us accountable, to make sure we keep promises we make to ourselves, to keep us from becoming distracted, and to give us a swift kick in the backside when it's needed. I call them Accountability Coaches. Some people call them mentors, but to me a mentor is someone older and more experienced than you who imparts some special wisdom that you don't possess.

It's wonderful if you can find a great mentor to be your Accountability Coach; great mentors are worth their weight in gold. But it's not critical. A good Accountability Coach is someone who understands what you're trying to accomplish in reintroducing your passion into your work and is not shy about making sure you keep your commitments to yourself. A great coach will call you with encouragement, listen to your gripes and self-doubt when you miss a goal or make a mistake, lend a different perspective to tough times, remind you of what you've really accomplished so far, and most important, NEVER let you quit.

Write down the names and contact information of people who would be great Accountability Coaches. You can have more than one, you know. Then call them and ask them to lunch. Explain what you're trying to do, and ask them if they would be willing to coach you. If they're like most folks, they'll be extremely flattered and happy to help.

OK, It's Day 21. Now What?

When you've got all that information down and refined to the point where you're happy with it, you're ready to implement your plan. There's not much more to say about that: just get going and make it happen!

After the 21st day of your first plan, take your Passion Journal (see below) and set aside some quiet time. This is the time you need to evaluate how you did during the past 21 days in making progress toward a professional life built around your passion. Review your notes for the past three weeks and ask yourself:

- How many of my goals did I hit?

- How many did I miss and why?

- What unforeseen obstacles got in my way?

- What was the best thing I achieved in the last 21 days?

- What was my biggest disappointment?

- How do I need to adjust my plan, if at all?

In the next chapter, you'll see a comprehensive checklist for reviewing every aspect of your 21-Day Passion Plan. But this will get you started. Ask and answer the questions, make any changes you need to make to your plan, and the next day, launch right into your next 21-Day Passion Plan. Then repeat. You're going to do this as long as it takes to make your vision a reality!

Start a Passion Journal

This is essential. Journaling is a wonderful way to track the evolution of your thoughts through time and see how the experience of pursuing your passion is changing you in ways you don't and can't expect. My suggestion is this: the day you complete your 21-Day Passion Plan, start your Passion Journal. It can be handwritten, an audio journal done on a digital recorder, or written on your computer in a word processing program. Whatever works best for you is fine. Personally, I think it's great to have a Passion Journal you can take with you wherever you go, so if you don't have a laptop computer or handheld recorder, you might want to keep your journal in an old-fashioned journal book, written by hand. I think it's kind of cool to make it a ceremonial thing and buy a beautiful leather-bound book and a first-class pen to write with. It makes journaling a special occasion.

Once you've got your journal ready, your job is simple. Start writing every day about the things you did to follow your Passion Plan, as well as anything you did during the day that's related to your pursuit of your passion. This means writing about the steps you took toward bringing your passion into your job, finding an Accountability Coach, or the progress you make toward adopting new habits. This last is particularly important. As you're trying to take on new habits and break old ones, keep to a new schedule and move toward change at the end of 21 days, your Passion Journal can be an invaluable way to "check yourself" and catch negative patterns of behavior before they progress too far.

For example, if one of your 21-day goals was the adoption of a new positive habit, yet you notice in your journal that on five days in a row you intended to engage in the positive habit but failed to do so, you'll see the pattern. You can then stop and say, "OK, what do I need to do so that I will adopt this good habit and not make excuses?" Then you can take proactive steps to turn things around.

Passion Journal Rules

Remember, you're not a dewy-eyed adolescent ranting about boyfriends or high school ennui here. You're a motivated adult with passion in your heart and specific goals for your journaling. So here are some ground rules to follow for maintaining your Passion Journal:

1. **Designate a set time for journaling each day.** In fact, if you can, designate a space as well where you will be undisturbed. Having "Passion Journal time" in each day will not only make you a more productive journaler, but it will become time you can look forward to as contemplative and healing. I know of people who journal in their cars after driving to a quiet spot, perhaps with a view, and writing where no one else can bother them.

2. **Review your journal every two weeks.** That's how you'll catch those nonproductive behaviors and stop yourself before you get too far. Go back and look over your entries, looking for patterns, negative self-talk and anything else you want to change.

3. **Be analytical.** Do more than describe what you did each day; analyze what you have done and why. This is the key to the experience: developing the self-knowledge to figure out why you do what you do and how changing that behavior can bring you closer to your passion.

4. **Note the steps you took forward and backward each day.** Your Passion Journal is a map of your journey, so it's going to be most valuable if in each day's entry, you track what you've done each day. At the end of your entry, write down the "forward steps" you took that day and any "backward steps" you might have taken, if any. Persisting in a new, positive habit is a forward step; feeling bad about yourself for having the nerve to have passion is a backward step.

5. **Don't edit yourself.** This is a highly personal record of your journey, not an English 101 assignment. You're not being graded on writing style. Don't cross things out or mark them as "stupid." Your goal is to write candidly and openly from the heart about how you're feeling in this process. There are no wrong answers.

6. **Rewrite your goals each day**. At the top of the page for each day's entry, rewrite your goals for your current 21-day plan. This will help them stay fresh in your mind and remind you of your desired destination.

7. **Mark every 21 days**. At the end of each 21-day period, make a note in your Passion Journal of the passage of time. More important, note what you have achieved in that 21 days. Did you meet your goals? Did you adopt a new schedule and new habits? What did you do to integrate your passion into your work? How did you do overall? How did you feel about the experience?

8. **Have fun.** Keeping a Passion Journal shouldn't be a chore. Enjoy the experience of learning about yourself and growing. Reward yourself for a month of successful journaling, draw cartoons or write down jokes—do whatever you can to make it fun.

Most of all, make Passion Journaling a lifetime pursuit. Even when you're fully in your passion, you should always keep your journal updated, if only to remind yourself where you've been. Ideally, once you begin your journal, it should be something you do for the rest of your days. Think of the amazement in twenty years when people read about the kind of person you used to be!

Create "Fail-Safes" For Yourself

Finally, we both know this isn't going to be easy. I can talk all I want about goal setting and plans and journals, but the fact is you're going to be making some pretty radical life transformations as you move toward your passion, and you won't always be successful. That's completely OK. Not a single person I know who has succeeded in taking his or her passion and making it the center of his or her life has done it without some backsliding and failure.

However, there is a way you can give yourself the "kick in the pants" that most of us need to get started with major changes in our lives. I call this building "fail-safes" into your 21-Day Passion Plan. What are fail-safes? They are actions that leave you no choice but to take further action, so you can't back out of your plan and say, "Oh, well, I'll go after my passion next week." No you won't. That excuse turns into procrastination, and then you're right back where you started, only five years older. Instead, use fail-safes to get you moving when your motivation fails.

Once you have your vision, core values and everything else that defines your passion in place, look at your situation. How can you jump-start yourself on the road to change? Be creative. When Hernando Cortez was exploring the New World in the sixteenth century, he burned his ships upon reaching land. Why? Because he didn't want to give his men (or himself) an easy way out, a quick passage back to Spain. They had two choices: conquer and survive, or fail and perish. That's what you're going to do: burn your ships. What can you do that forces you to take radical action and make changes? Here are some ideas:

- Give notice at your job. This is a big one, and not for everyone. But if you need to break free to pursue your passion, giving 30 days might be just the kick you need to finish that business plan and start that company of your own.

- End a relationship with a colleague who is negative or makes you feel inferior. Walk away and start anew. It can be very empowering.

- Telling others what you're doing. When you announce to colleagues that you're embarking on your journey to chase your passion, you turn them into de facto Accountability Coaches. It can be very motivating indeed to have co-workers asking, "So Gary, what happened to that passion you were so fired up about?"

- Giving away or selling possessions. The act of divestiture goes back centuries to many different traditional peoples. In every case, the meaning of the act is the same: you are washing your hands of the excess baggage of your life, moving beyond it. So if your passion is fitness, you might sell your car, forcing you to walk or cycle and thereby moving your fitness goals forward. If your passion is to write your novel, give your home computer to a local school so you don't waste more time surfing the Internet, and buy a typewriter. You get the picture.

- You can probably think of a dozen fail-safes that apply to your life. Write them down in detail: what you'll do, when, why, and what the repercussions will be. Then make them part of your 21-Day Passion Plan, but keep them in your holster unless you really need them. You'll know right away: if Day 1 of your 21-day plan comes along and you find yourself making excuses, you might need to pull out a fail-safe and give yourself the rocket boost of irreversible action. It's amazing what you'll do when you give yourself no choice!

Now, let's jump ahead to the next step in this process. Once you have your Passion Plan in order, down on paper and integrated into your life, it's time to execute your plan and make fantastic things happen in your life. A big part of that is monitoring your progress as the days pass and making sure you're going in the direction of your greatest passion, purpose and joy. Let's look at how you'll do that.

Chapter Eight

Execute Your Plan Every Day

Nothing great has been and nothing great can be accomplished without passion.
— *Georg Wilhelm Friedrich Hegel, German philosopher*

The great psychologist Abraham Maslow created the concept of the "self-actualized" person. Someone who is self-actualized has completely accepted who he or she is, positive and negative attributes included in equal measure. This person has forgiven himself or herself for any faults and makes the most of his or her strengths. As a result, such a person is magnetic, inspirational and wise, often advancing the human condition by virtue of great genius or insight. Self-actualization is beyond self-esteem; it's the total realization of one's mental, emotional and spiritual potential.

About the self-actualized individual, Maslow had this to say:

A musician must make music, an artist must paint, a poet must write, if he is to be at peace with himself. What a man can be, he must be. This is the need we may call self-actualization... It refers to man's desire for fulfillment, namely to the tendency for him to become actually in what he is potentially: to become everything that one is capable of becoming..."

As examples of this exalted state, Maslow cited people like Abraham Lincoln, Thomas Jefferson, Ben Franklin, Pablo Picasso and Eleanor Roosevelt. These are human beings who make us proud to share the same genetic material. They seem to be linked to some higher order of consciousness, to be able to achieve things that most mere mortals can only dream of. And yet they are men and women like you and me. What's the difference?

I'm delighted to tell you that there is no difference between you and these immortals. As you embark on the journey to discover your passion, you are on the road to becoming self-actualized. Your passion is the fullest expression of who you are and what you can achieve. According to Maslow, the two keys to self-actualization are *self-exploration* and *action*. You are already well into the first, with the insight and wisdom you've gained from the process of uncovering your buried passion and the values behind it. Eventually, you will turn that knowledge into action. The deeper your self-knowledge, the more effective your action and the greater your self-actualized potential. So the more you know, the more you can achieve. I urge you right now, at this moment, to commit to completely dropping any remaining barriers you might have to inner truths or self-realization. You'll find the results far more rewarding.

Never Doubt Your Dreams

I have learned never to doubt my wife Cherisse. She dreams big. Dreams are intended to be lived out with others. They are what life is made of, and those with faith and perseverance make their dreams reality. I'm married to one of those people.

Cherisse had always dreamed of swimming with dolphins, and she had her mind and heart set on making it happen. She knew that the fastest way to make a dream come true is to visualize it. Soon I began seeing pictures of dolphins on the refrigerator door, in the bathroom, on the computer. When I asked her about them, she'd say, "Soon, honey. I want to see my reality before it becomes my reality."

Weeks later, I arrived home from a speaking engagement to find her waiting for me with exciting news. She'd found a resort in Hawaii where you could actually swim with dolphins. "It's called the Hilton Waikoloa Resort on the Big Island," she announced with a huge smile. Now, keep in mind that I had just come from a conference where I had told people their dreams could come true if they had the faith and desire to make them happen. But at home, Mr. Motivator became Mr. I Don't Think So. It is hard work to practice what you preach.

"Hawaii?" I said. "You've got to be kidding." At the time I was working on some new marketing materials, and it was taking every dime I had. She looked me straight in the eye and said, "We are going on this trip for free."

"Did we win something?"

"No."

"Is it a gift?"

"No."

"So how are we going to get there?"

My amazing wife smiled. "I'll let you know when I figure that part out," she said and walked away. Nothing stops her, my Cherisse.

A few days later she told me she had called the resort and spoken with the general manager. She had convinced the manager of the Hilton resort to let us come to the hotel free for a week by offering my services as a speaker while we were there. Let me tell you, one night at this place would have been beyond our budget, but we were going to get a week in paradise! This was too good to be true... then it occurred to me that it might be. I asked her what the catch was.

Innocently, she said, "I promised them if they weren't completely satisfied with your presentation, you'd pay for your entire stay."

"Are you out of your MIND?" I had just seen financial ruin before my eyes. I began wondering if those marriage vows included an escape clause for being made an accessory to fraud.

Calm as ever, Cherisse explained. The hotel wanted me to speak on the subject of corporate mergers and teamwork. The Hilton had just bought the property from the Hyatt Corporation, and blending new management with existing management was, as always, a challenge. This was a good subject, but there was just one eensy-weensy problem: *I didn't know anything about corporate mergers!*

"Tell me you did not agree to what I think you agreed to," I wailed.

She looked at me with the confidence of a general sending a young soldier into battle. "I told them that was your specialty," she said.

"But honey, it's not my specialty," I said.

"It will be by the time we get there."

I prepared. I studied. I spoke. I knew I would do anything to help Cherisse's dream come true. Today we have a framed photo of my wife and me swimming with dolphins in Hawaii, looking as happy as can be. We have been back every year since. Robin Graff, the hotel manager to whom my wife "stretched" the truth, has become a dear friend of the family.

Dreamers always see what could be rather than what is. A passionaut is, by definition, a dreamer. Cherisse saw herself swimming with dolphins; it was her passion. She saw what could be, what would be and what should be. You will learn to do the same with your dreams—to have faith in them and trust their truth.

A Lifetime Commitment

As you're no doubt realizing, the pursuit of passion is not some pie-in-the-sky endeavor where you sit and meditate in a field of flowers. It's work. And it should be. You're making not just a life change but a paradigm shift—a move away from your old belief system that dictated that you had to settle for where you are instead of striving for something more. That's an effort perhaps greater than anything you've ever done in your life. But it's going to be worth it!

Let's consider what you've achieved so far, whether you've followed along by carrying out each step, or are reading the entire book and intend to go back later and complete the steps. You've come to a greater understanding of what passion is and what it can do in your life. You've identified your single most important passion and the values that underlie your life. You've determined your short-term and long-term goals and figured out what you need to do to bring your passion into your professional life. And most recently, you've seen the blueprint for a practical daily plan you can use to gradually flow your passion into your work. That's a lot of progress, and it's time to make more.

You're in motion. Now you need to stay in motion. Passion is a lifetime commitment; it's not enough simply to make lists and take a few steps and then slack off and vow to "get back to it later." Take it from me: if you approach your passion in a start-and-stop fashion, you'll spin your wheels for years and get nowhere. It's very easy to lose your momentum and allow the demands of daily work and home life to pull your attention from your passion. That's why we created the 21-Day plan, and that's why in this chapter, I'm going to walk you through how to monitor and check your progress using real metrics, concrete measurements of how you're doing.

Seeing Results

Assuming you have started following your 21-Day plan, you should have started seeing some results. That means you should be experiencing some or all of the following:

- Talking to staff or colleagues about your passion

- Beginning to transform your workspace in subtle ways

- Feeling more enthusiasm for your work

- Being more energized at the end of the day

You may also find yourself experiencing something common to my audiences: noticing things related to your passion that you did not notice before. This is the effect of your brain's *reticular activating system,* a part of your brain that makes your mind notice things once you are aware of them. You know how when you buy a new car, suddenly you notice lots of other people driving that car? That's your reticular activator doing its job: making meaningful connections. You should be seeing that effect if you're firmly centered in your passion.

If you're starting to see even subtle results, you're well on your way to becoming a passion-centered professional. But small personal perceptions can be deceiving; you can't always trust your own sense of your progress, as anyone who *thinks* they're dieting and losing weight but actually cheating and not losing a pound can tell you. So we're going to create an accountability system that will tell you if you're really making the progress you think you are over time. The Passion Checklist, which you will complete every 21 days, will keep you grounded and focused on what you need to do and prevent you from being sidetracked. Previously, you were in the *launch* phase of your passion plan. Now you're getting into *maintenance*. Let's do it.

The Passion Checklist

Every 21 days, you will complete this checklist and act on whatever it suggests. I recommend either photocopying and enlarging the pages of this book, or entering the material into a spreadsheet or word processing program so you can reproduce the checklist and use it whenever you like.

Your Vision Statement

Go back and review your vision statement and answer the following questions:

- Are your actions since beginning your passion plan in line with your vision?

- Is your vision statement on target, or is it proving to be different in practice?

- Do you need to revise your vision statement? How?

Core Values

Your core values are the engine behind all the changes you will be making to blend your passion with your professional life. Take an honest look at your actions over the last 21 days and answer:

- Have you been adhering to your core values?

- Do some of your values need to change? If so, in what way?

Changes

Passion pursuit is about change. You're going to be experiencing change at a rapid pace, more rapid than the vast majority of people are accustomed to. That's because unlike most folks, who tend to just react to change as it comes to them, you're instigating it. This is both more rewarding and more challenging. It's thought that the average person can cope productively with no more than three concurrent changes in his or her life, one in each of the three main areas of change: Personal (who you are), Vocational (what you do) and Environmental (the world around you).

By bringing your passion to life you may be provoking multiple changes in all those areas: relationships, your health (from stress), your income, how you spend your time and so on. It's important to monitor the effect of these changes on your emotional and mental state so you can stay on task.

- What has changed so far?

- Which changes have been positive or achieved the results you desired?

- Which changes have been unsuccessful?

- How do you feel about the results of these changes so far?

- What else do you need to change?

Your Schedule

Your use of time will likely change as you bring your passion to life. You will probably need to make "holes" in your life to allow you to get into your passion, whether that means shopping for furnishings for your personal space or taking lessons in something.

- Have you had to make changes in your schedule?

- What aspects of your new schedule are working?

- What aspects are not working?

- What do you need to do to make necessary holes in your life?

Your Habits

As we have discussed before, our habits define us. The actions we engage in every day determine how we look and feel, how much we earn, how we spend our time, and how strong our relationships are, just for starters. But does that mean you're a slave of your habits with no ability to change? Of course not. I'm not deterministic. You have the will and the means to re-train your mind and change your habits. It's not easy, but that's what the process of bringing out your passion it about. You're changing your habits as we speak, and that's a gradual process. This part of the checklist is about tracking and encouraging that personal transformation of what we do every day.

- What unproductive habits have you broken?

- What positive new habits are you on the way to acquiring?

- What do you need to do to begin acquiring other positive habits?

- What do you need to do to break negative habits you still have?

Taking Your Passion to Work

Here's where the rubber meets the road. How have you been able bring your passion into your office environment and to your working activity?

- In what ways have you been able to bring your passion into your work?

- What ways have you tried that haven't worked out?

- What has been the response of others to your efforts?

- What will you do next to bring passion to work?

- What else do you need to do to transform your working life?

- Does your experience suggest that you might need to change your profession or get a different job?

Your Bag of Tricks

Earlier we talked about the tricks you can use to get yourself moving toward your passion, even if you're reluctant or nervous about taking action. In the beginning, results matter more than how you get them; just like with weight loss, you need fast results to motivate you to keep going.

- What tricks have you used to keep yourself going?

- Which ones worked and why?

- Which ones fell flat and why?

- What brainstorms do you have for future tricks?

Your Goals

This checklist focuses on your short-term goals. Since you're in your early stages of passion integration, your early progress will set the stage for your future, larger goals. After you've been engaged in the pursuit of your passion for a year or two, your small goals will be achieved and you probably won't need this checklist. But for now, it's essential to keep your eye on the ball.

- What was your short-term goal?

- Did you make progress toward that goal?

- Why or why not?

- What steps did you take toward the goal?

- Did you set the right short-term goal?

- Do you need to revise your short-term goal, and in what way?

- What do you think your new goal might need to become?

Your Accountability Coach

As part of your plan, you needed to select at least one Accountability Coach, a person who will call you on any excuses and hold you responsible for meeting your goals.

- How did you rely on your Accountability Coach?

- What did your coach do?

- What did he or she not do that you needed?

- What do you expect to need from your coach in the next 21 days?

- Might you need to make a change in your coach?

- Which people might be good alternatives?

Using Your Checklist

After each 21-day cycle, complete your checklist with as much detail and honesty as you can. Once you're done, ask yourself some basic questions. How am I doing so far? During the last 21 days, did I get closer to bringing my passion fully into my profession? Did I make positive changes in my lifestyle, schedule and habits? Am I making progress?

Those are broad, general questions, but the checklist will aid you in coming up with specific answers that will guide your future progress. As you go through the 21-day cycles, also be sure to keep each checklist, because as time passes you'll want to go back and review past checklists against your current one. This is essential because you don't want to fall into non-productive patterns. Together with your Passion Journal, reviewing your checklist from time to time will keep you on the mark toward your goal.

Forgiving Yourself

Finally, a word or two about forgiveness. Namely, forgiving yourself when you fall short of your goals. Because you will. It's inevitable. And if you're a driven person who has always succeeded at whatever you tried (as many of my clients tend to be), you're probably going to beat yourself up over it. Well, stop. You're not perfect. You're trying to effect massive change on a state of being that's got a great deal of momentum behind it—that is, your life. It's not easy.

When you find that you spent a 21-day period too busy or tired to follow most or all of the steps in your Passion Plan, your only response should be, "Why?" Try to figure out what it was that stopped you from making progress, so you can identify ways to help yourself and your Accountability Coach be more effective in the next 21 days. Beyond that, let it go. If you're trying to lose weight, you're going to have a day when you just can't resist having a bacon cheeseburger. But there's no use wearing sackcloth and ashes afterward; it won't get you back on your fitness program. All you can do is forgive yourself for a one-time aberration, get up the next morning and go to the gym.

Passion is the same way. You're trying to get your life in shape. If you have a 21-day stretch where you don't take much constructive action, vow to do better the next time. Set up some fail-safes so you won't have a choice but to act. Figure out what you learned about yourself during the previous cycle (there's always something). If you need motivation, talk to your coach, a mentor or a pastor. It's not the end of the world. Don't act like it is. Remember, the fact that you're reading this book at all means you've taken a greater leap toward your ideal life than most people ever will!

Moving Ahead

This completes the Passion Process. From this point on, you've got the tools you need to begin discovering what your passion has in store for you. Simply follow the steps I've outlined in the last five chapters:

- Determine what your single most powerful passion is.

- Decide what core values define who you are and how your passion can serve those values.

- Create a set of passion-centered career goals, keeping them realistic and focusing most on short-term goals that you can achieve in the next year.

- Go through the visioning process and develop a concise, powerful vision statement for how you see your life evolving as your passion becomes part of it.

- Create your 21-Day Passion Plan to give yourself concrete steps to follow to work your passion into your profession.

- Use the checklist to monitor your progress through each 21-day cycle.

The process will uncover levels of self-insight, fear, love and knowledge that you may not have explored since you were an undergraduate, if ever. Enjoy it. Most people don't ever get the chance to earn such valuable self-awareness. Savor it. You're on the road to a sweeter, richer existence.

Now let's move on to the bigger challenge: bringing your passion and your work together in the real world of office relationships, power dynamics, deadlines, and competition.

Part III

The Passionate Workplace

Chapter Nine

Communicating Your Passion at Work

We can no more explain a passion to a person who has never ex-
perienced it than we can explain light to the blind.

—*T.S. Eliot*

In 1955, psychologists Joseph Luft and Harry Ingham created
a metaphorical tool for understanding self-perception and relationships with others called the Johari Window. The Window consists
of four quadrants in which are placed different traits or behaviors
of the person being analyzed. They are:

- The **Arena**, which contains traits of the person that both the
  subject and other people are aware of.

- The **Façade,** which holds the traits that the person being analyzed knows about but other people don't know about.

- The **Blind Spot**, where you'll find traits that the subject doesn't
  know about but other people perceive.

- The **Unknown**, the home to qualities or behaviors that neither
  the subject nor others know of.

It's a powerful tool for discovering not only the truths about
ourselves that we keep from others, but how others perceive us in
ways we may not be aware of. I reference the Johari Window at this

point because now that we're through the painstaking steps necessary to identify, understand and develop your passion, it's time for the next phase in your transformation. That means getting out of the theoretical and actually introducing your passion into your professional life.

When you do this, you will be introducing a side of yourself into your working environment that those who work with you—which includes not just staff, but colleagues and patients or clients—may have never seen. You have been maintaining a façade for years by not revealing your inner longings to them, and you may have been unaware of your own need for your passion's expression. Or it's possible that others saw signs of your passion in your behavior, but said nothing, leaving you in the blind spot on the presumption that talking to you about it was none of their business.

Whether your past handling of your passion was right or wrong is immaterial. What matters is now. You're going to begin the process of folding your passionate pursuit into your work life in the way a chef folds ingredients into a mix. Hopefully, the results are smooth and effortless, but they may not be. It doesn't matter. As long as you are aware of how others regard your abrupt shift to a passion-centered life, you can deal with the turbulence that can result.

Get Outside Your Own Head

Abrupt? But this has been roiling around in your mind and gut for years! True, but you weren't sharing it with anybody. To the people who make up your professional circle, you're probably the rock-steady physician or stockbroker or corporate officer who's predictable as the sunset. To them, your transformation is going to be as sudden as a cloudburst. It's going to surprise them, make some of them wonder if you're suffering from stress or even headed for a nervous breakdown. I've seen it, trust me. Revelation is rare for all people, and the older you are the rarer it is. When you show up for work one day filled with passionate energy, you might find people touching you on the upper arm and asking with deep concern in their eyes, "Are you all right?"

I think this is hysterically funny, because you've never been better! You're in the process of finally becoming who you knew you needed to be. But you can't say that. As I've said before, passion will always encounter opposition. Most folks won't get what you're going through. A few will envy it. It's vital that you get out of your own head and see things from the perspective of others—get out of your blind spot and become more aware of how you appear. They want to trust you, and if you're seen as being unstable, they won't. So you must approach your transition—your *rebirth* into a new style of professional existence, if you will—with prudence and discretion.

You may be thinking, "Hey, I own the practice/office/company, so who cares what other people think?" You should. Nobody succeeds alone, and unless you're one of the few people reading this book who's ready to ditch it all and road trip to the northern California redwoods to spend your life making dulcimers, you're going to have to continue working with the people in your sphere. You need your reputation. So you need a plan, and that's what this chapter is all about: having a plan to integrate your passion into your work life gradually, wisely and farsightedly.

Save the Environment

Your goal here is simple: you want to enlist the people in your workplace as partners in your passion-centered development. Ideally, you want to fire up *their* passions as well so they can share your journey. You're trying to create a more passion-centered environment for everyone, because that means less resistance for you in bringing your passion to your work in multiple ways. That's a Passion Principle:

> *The optimal passion pursuit involves not just you, but everyone around you.*

What does a passionate working environment look and feel like? These are some of the hallmarks I've seen in my work:

- People come to work with more energy and enthusiasm.

- They bring new ideas to their superiors immediately because they're confident they'll be recognized.

- Communication becomes more open because everyone understands that they have a passion.

- There's less envy and rivalry.

- There's more healthy competition.

- Lifestyle tends to replace money as the major gauge of job satisfaction.

- Everyone feels more respected and listened to.

Here's the interesting thing: I've seen these changes occur even if *nothing* else changes about the business except that everyone is open to hearing and expressing their passions! The company or practice might change zero about working conditions, pay scales, training methods, meeting styles, work hours, and so on, but people still feel more positive and valued. Talk about a cheap productivity boost!

Your goal in bringing your passion to work is not just to express your passion and get the approval and understanding of other people. It's also to make your passion infectious, so others will feel inspired enough to begin thinking about their own passions and joining with you on your journey.

Talk Ain't Cheap

Bringing items related to your passion to your workplace is easy. Transforming your workspace to evoke that thing you're in love with? Piece of cake. Let's face it, the real work in this part of your passion journey is talking to the people you work with about the changes you're experiencing. It's especially difficult because you're going to get a wide range of reactions that are not always predictable. Subordinates may voice their approval but be afraid to tell you what they think because of their position. Colleagues may either cheer you for doing what they've always thought about doing, or secretly envy you. Or they may think you're nuts and try to "talk you down from the ledge." Superiors may simply not get it at all and think you're looking for ways to shirk your responsibilities.

We'd love to think that our passion shows in our faces and is crystal clear to everyone. We all do this. I call it "presumed transparency." You think that because something is obvious to you that it will also be obvious to those around you. Trust me, it won't be. You've got a job to do here: to talk with all the different kinds of people who interact with you in your working life and help them understand what you're trying to do in nurturing your passion. Ideally, you want them to share your enthusiasm and even get on board. You'll settle for them just staying out of your way. What you don't want are people trying to sabotage you. In this section, we're going talk about how to talk about your passion.

The "No Opinion" Zone

You need a communication plan as you venture into this new territory, but it doesn't have to be complicated. First of all, understand how things are likely to proceed. Initially, you'll introduce changes to your working life. You'll fill your office with memorabilia related to your passion, start taking off at 5:01 to take a class, or stay late to work on the novel you've wanted to write since you were eighteen. For a while, nobody will notice. But after a few days or a few weeks, they'll notice not your actions, but *you*. Your demeanor, your carriage, your energy level. That's when the questions will begin.

There are a few good rules you should follow for talking with people about your passionate new reality:

- **Stay positive.** Don't talk about the negative forces that compelled you to pursue your passion. You might start rumors that you're unhappy. Instead, focus on phrases like, "I wanted to stretch myself" or "I've been wanting to branch out for a while."

- **Don't solicit opinions.** After you tell people about your passion, don't ask them what they think of it. You shouldn't care, and you're inviting criticism that may make you doubt yourself. Instead...

- **Ask them about their passions.** When you've told your story, ask the listener if he or she has a passion. As a journalist friend of mine says, people love to tell their stories. Invite others to share their passions with you, and they may open up to you in ways you never thought possible.

- **Don't predict the future.** Don't speculate where your passion pursuit might lead five or ten years down the line. You might create expectations you can't meet or make people think you're preparing to leave your company or practice. Stick to what you're doing, not what it might mean.

Above all, pick and choose the people with whom you share your passion. With some, you might choose to volunteer information, while you might wait for others to ask. I suggest making a "watch list" of all the people in your workplace and determining which ones you do not want to engage in lengthy explanations about your passion experience. Such people are typically those who are habitually negative, workaholics who think there's nothing but the office, super-skeptics who tend to pooh-pooh anything that seems "touchy feely," and people who you think might try to sabotage you.

Of course, people in your workspace will hear about your passion through the grapevine, so you won't keep it a secret. But you don't have to give details or get in arguments with people who will do nothing but harm your confidence. With the other people, keep in mind this important Passion Principle:

> *Your passion should inspire those who*
> *can be inspired. If it doesn't, then you're*
> *probably not living your true passion.*

Talking Points for "What's Up With You?"

You're going to hear a lot of questions from a lot of people, and it doesn't matter whether you instigate the conversation or field questions out of the blue. As you progress in bringing your passion into your workplace, you'll need to adopt evolving strategies to turn questions into productive conversations that leave you and the other person feeling heard, respected and even inspired.

Understand that despite all my warnings, most of the people in your workplace will genuinely be curious about what you're doing and happy for you that you've found something that enhances your life. But just in case, it's great to have some strategies in mind for dealing with the ongoing questions. These are some talking points I have found very helpful in turning the passion conversations in a positive direction:

- **Greater profitability**—Especially if you're dealing with a superior or co-operator of a practice, make sure to emphasize that passion may help you increase productivity and may also help others do the same. This is a powerful argument for getting people on your side.

- **Detail your passion**—If trust exists, go ahead and share the origin of your passion with the person. Tell them how you arrived at your "Aha" moment, share where your passion came from, and so on. Flatter the listener with intimate details of your journey. Who knows, you might inspire someone else to chase his or her passion!

- **Ask them about their passions**—This is always a winner. Everyone, even the crustiest old veteran, has a passion. People love to be asked to tell their stories, and even if they won't share theirs with you, they'll be more inclined to respect your journey if you have the courtesy to ask after theirs.

- **Talk about lifestyle**—All of us crave a lifestyle with more peace and freedom, more time with family, or a greater chance to pursue cherished hobbies. Tell your listener about the changes you hope to bring about in your lifestyle.

- **Talk about control of your time**—This is a big issue. Time is the one commodity we can never replenish, and we're all trying to make the most of ours. Talk about how you're trying to change how you use your time with your passion as the key. The listener will relate to your efforts, because it's a given that he or she would like to make more from his or her time as well. You can even exchange ideas.

- **Share your goals**—Tell the listener about the specific goals you have in mind for your future. This can be tricky; you may not want to tell your boss about your goal to leave and start your own company competing with your current employer. But if your goals are to get in shape, build a log house or climb K2, talk about it. People love lofty goals and are inspired by them. Become a source of inspiration!

- **Talk about giving back**—Finally, share the ways in which you will use your passion as a springboard to give back to your community or the world. You know the kind of people this information will affect: the activists who already volunteer themselves. Tell them about the organizations you'll give to, the charities you might start, the foundation you'd like to launch, and so on.

How to Talk to The Five Types

If you think I'm paying a lot of attention to how to communicate your passion to the people in your professional life, there's a reason. Nothing will derail your passion train like a work environment that's unsupportive or hostile to what you're doing. So learning how to talk to people about your passion is a survival skill. I've broken down the kinds of individuals you'll have to deal with into five groups, each of which has different needs based on common characteristics that I've seen. No two people are the same, of course, so you'll have to rely on your own insight into each person's character and personality to refine your communication. The five types:

- **Superiors**—The key to talking to superiors about your passion is doing so without threatening them. They may think you are planning to leave or that you covet their jobs. Make it clear that you are pursing your passion because you want to enjoy your working life more and you see it increasing your productivity.

- **Subordinates**—With employees or people below you on the organizational totem pole, there is a danger that being too effusive about sharing your passion with them will make them lose respect for you. You might come across as having your head in the clouds or being focused on something other than work. This can result in subordinate performance suffering because they think you no longer care. Avoid this by making it clear your work is still your number-one concern and framing your pursuit of your passion as a way to improve your professional life.

- **Colleagues**—These are your equals, and they may share your feelings of dissatisfaction or ennui. That doesn't mean they will support you. Colleagues can range from supportive to actively oppositional when it comes to your passion. Gauge colleagues case by case: if you suspect they are after your job, share little. If they face the same feelings you're dealing with, tell them you've discovered a wonderful secret. In general, use your own judgment. Be aware that colleagues are the most likely to envy you.

- **Customers**—I suggest being very circumspect about your passion with customers (used here to mean everything from medical patients to legal clients). They are looking to you to care about nothing but their needs, so they may see your passion as a distraction. If you know some customers well enough to know they will appreciate your passion, share it on a case-by-case basis.

- **Friends**—Some people in your working environment may be friends. I suggest with friends you be the most honest, telling them that you need your passion to reinvigorate your work after years of the same challenges. They will understand and appreciate your confiding in them, and if asked will probably share their own expressed and unfulfilled passions.

Ask and Keep Asking

Sometimes when a person at work quizzes you about the changes in your behavior, it's a cry to be heard. I've seen this a lot. Some people don't want to talk about a passion directly, because they are afraid of ridicule. But they'll ask you about yours and use it as an opening to find out more. What are you doing? How are you making the leap they have yet to make? When this happens, I find the best thing you can do is ask questions.

Most of us love to talk about ourselves. But when you do that, you demonstrate that you only care about yourself. By asking questions, you show through your actions and an investment of your time that you care about the other person. In this way you might find an ally in passion, someone who could be priceless in helping you find your calling. It's possible; you never know. Plus, you might learn something.

Try what I call playing a game of "verbal tennis." If you sense that the person really wants to tell you about his passion, every time he speaks in conversation, respond with a question about him. Here's an example:

Man: You've been making some changes.

You: What made you notice?

Man: Oh, I don't know.

You: Have you been thinking about making some changes of your own?

Man: Yes, as a matter of fact I have.

You: What kind of changes?

Man: Oh, I'm really not sure...

You: Well, what would you like to be doing every day?

Man: I'd like to work fewer hours and spend more time with my family.

You: I didn't know you had a family. How many kids?

Man: Two girls and a boy. How about you?

You: Two sons. What do you enjoy doing most with them?

And so on. See how easy it was to turn the conversation from being about you to being about your colleague? People love to talk about themselves, and you've just opened the door to greater communication. You might make a friend, gain a business ally or meet someone who will change your life. You can do this in the office, at a networking event or even on a plane. Just ask questions and show the other person you care. You may be surprised at what you learn.

Know When to Lie Low

Sometimes talking about your passion is the worst thing you can do, especially if you're not the boss. When you're in an environment where you feel that your pursuit of passion will not be understood or will be greeted with resentment, keep quiet. This can be difficult if bringing your passion into your profession means bringing visible reminders of it to your workplace. If that's the case, you may want to reconsider how you express your passion from nine to five. Instead of trumpeting your newly discovered life purpose, you might want to downplay it. Instead, let the changes you exhibit on the job do your talking—your improved productivity, your more positive attitude. Then when someone asks you how you're doing it, just smile and shrug and enjoy your secret.

There are some warning signs that you may work in a passion-unfriendly environment:

- The powers that be are antagonistic toward original or iconoclastic thinking.

- Individuality or creativity are looked down upon.

- In-house communication is poor or nonexistent.

- Morale is consistently terrible.

When I have encountered this type of environment in a coaching or consulting situation, I respond by developing strategies to transform the entire organization and make it more receptive to people who are on their passion journey. That's probably not an option for you at the outset, so it's best to be circumspect. Even if you're the boss, your time to transform your organization will come later.

The Crazy Index

It's inevitable. When you start telling people about what you've discovered and how you're changing how you approach your work to chase some passion you've had since you were a kid, you're going to hear it: "You're crazy." As I said earlier in the book, this can be an eviscerating moment for some people. Remember, passion in its early form is fragile; it often takes only one person's disdain to discourage someone and send him or her crawling back to the life he or she used to lead. But if you understand what being called crazy really means, you'll learn to cherish the words.

Reflect on these quotes:

Great spirits have always encountered violent opposition from mediocre minds.

—Albert Einstein

Some people never go crazy, what truly horrible lives they must live.
—Charles Bukowski

A man who is "of sound mind" is one who keeps the inner madman under lock and key.

—Paul Valery

The distance between insanity and genius is measured only by success.

—Bruce Feirstein

No great genius has ever existed without some touch of madness.
—Aristotle

Crazy people who are productive are geniuses. Crazy people who
are rich are eccentric. Crazy people who are neither productive nor rich
are just plain crazy. Geniuses and crazy people are both out in the
middle of a deep ocean; geniuses swim, crazy people drown. Most of us
are sitting safely on the shore. Take a chance and get your feet wet.
—Michael J. Gelb

The point should be obvious: since the beginning of civilization innovative thinkers, creative geniuses and pioneers have been called crazy. Galileo and Copernicus were persecuted as heretics. Einstein was called insane by many after publishing his papers on relativity. Thomas Edison was considered a crank until he actually invented a light bulb that worked. If you've been called crazy, delusional, immature or misguided by anyone in your workplace, take it as a compliment.

More importantly, take being called crazy as a sign that you're on the right track with your passion. I call it the Crazy Index. The Index says that the more people who say "You're crazy" when you tell them about your passion, the more in the bulls-eye you are with what you're doing. Folks who have not had the transformative experience you have had are likely to regard what you're doing as nuts; they can't understand because they are still in a pre-passion mindset. It's as if you have passed through a door and they're still trapped outside, peering through the window. When you radiate passion and purpose and electricity that confounds their expectations, that's confirmation that you have indeed undergone a transformative experience. You're on the right track, not playing it safe.

I've actually created a Crazy Index based on the number of times you hear that you're off your rocker. It's partially in fun, but also kind of serious:

Crazy Index

HOW OFTEN YOU HEAR YOU'RE CRAZY	WHAT IT MEANS
1-2 times	Your passion is solid and apparent
3-4 times	You're a passion evangelist
5-6 times	You have the power to transform your organization from within
6+ times	You're so crazy you're a prophet!

So when a colleague or employee tells you, "Man, you've really gone off the deep end," you can smile inwardly and think, "You bet I have." Wear it as a badge of honor.

Take Credit for the Results of Your Passion

I'm not going to go further into people's responses to your passion declaration and how you can deal with them. There are as many responses as there are people, and you'll know best how to deal with the people you work with. But there's another issue at hand: how to deal with the way that your passion affects your work performance. Some of the people I coach are inclined to soft-pedal their achievements, but I say do the opposite: take credit for what your passion helps you accomplish.

As you come into your passion and express it at work, you're going to notice improvements in the various metrics by which you judge your success. You may see your income increasing, sales improving, your productivity rising, your morale climbing, even your energy levels looking better. In the end, these changes will show up on the bottom line for your company or practice as more revenue, more effective competition, and/or greater market share. In effect, your passion will produce results that no one has seen before.

When that occurs, don't be afraid to blow your own horn and let people know you were responsible, and let them know why: you were fueled by your passion. False humility is the last refuge of the incompetent. Stand up and take credit for what you've done. Not to do so makes you appear disingenuous, and it also denies you one of the pleasures of passion: enjoying your successes. This is a Passion Principle:

> *Take credit for what your passion helps you achieve, or you'll appear phony.*

Allowing yourself to bask in the glory of better work performance can really compensate for the confusion, envy or stupid comments you may have endured when you first "came out of the passion closet" at your workplace.

Find a Confidante

Last but certainly not least, it's essential that you have at least one person at your workplace who can be your "passion partner." This is a person who "gets it"—someone to whom you can talk about your passion openly and honestly, someone who understands the journey you're on and respects what you're trying to do. Since you really have no way of knowing how people will react to your pursuit of passion, it's important that you have at least one person who can be a sanctuary for you.

This person will probably be a colleague or friend, someone who is on the same level as you, another physician, attorney, or co-level executive. He or she will see himself or herself as your equal, able to give advice and share wisdom. But a confidante can be anyone, from a loyal assistant to a great boss. How will you know when you've found yours? In my experience, you'll just know. You'll talk about your passion to this person, and his or her eyes will light up. You know your confidante understands.

Bottom line: every work environment is different. You will encounter a galaxy of reactions to your passion pursuit, from total indifference to incomprehension to scorn to jealousy to enthusiasm and delight. But you will find more support than censure, and more people who will ask you "How can I do that?" than "Are you out of your mind?" Have a plan in mind for how you'll deal with questions, deflect negative reactions, and inspire others to embrace the path you're on. In the end, the results will speak for themselves.

Passion Principles from this chapter:

> *The optimal passion pursuit involves not just you, but everyone around you.*

> *Your passion should inspire those who can be inspired. If it doesn't, then you're probably not living your true passion.*

> *Take credit for what your passion helps you achieve, or you'll appear phony.*

Chapter Ten

Who's In Charge?

I think that, as life is action and passion, it is required of a man that he should share the passion and action of his time at peril of being judged not to have lived.

—*Oliver Wendell Holmes*

We're nearly at the end of our journey together. I hope it's been a fulfilling one. I've presented you with many challenges, and with luck you've been able to embrace the idea of passion and to make some progress. My intent is not to walk you along your life-long passion path, but to give you a solid start and help you develop the skills you'll need to direct your own progress toward fully realizing your passion.

However, I'm not going to leave you on your own without covering one more crucial area of passion-centered professionalism: what you should do when you're the boss and your work environment just isn't receptive to your dreams. Talking about your passion with others and trying to inspire them is one thing, but what if you communicate what's going on in your soul and no one cares, or some actively try to sabotage you? If you're a doctor or psychologist with your own practice, the broker in a real estate office, or the founder of a tax accounting firm, it's hard to just walk away. People depend on you. You've built something and you may not feel free to chuck it like so much garbage. What do you do?

Not to worry; you have options. Remember that I told you "passion creates your position." Well, here's another Passion Principle to learn:

> *Your position can also empower you*
> *to pursue your passion.*

If you're the man or woman at the top, you have the ability to create change in ways no one else can—to transform your business and make it a place that welcomes passionate people. There are many questions to ask and many possible paths to do this, and that's what we'll go over in this, our final chapter together.

The Passion Parachute

In probably half of the James Bond movies ever made, not to mention a raft of knockoff films, you'll find a souped-up sporty car with some interesting "options." One of these may be an ejector or escape seat, modeled after the emergency ejection system in fighter jets. The driver presses a button, the roof detaches, an explosive charge detonates and the driver is thrown into the air and clear of the car, in theory floating safely to the ground by parachute. Of course, he also gets the girl and looks killer in a tux.

Imagine that you bring your passion to your workplace and the worst possible thing happens: people are openly hostile to what you're doing. Even if you're self-employed in a contractor situation —as many mortgage brokers, insurance brokers and financial advisors are—your "company" may see your passion pursuit as a way to slack off and neglect your work. If things get terrible (and I have seen it happen), you may need to pull the cord on your "passion parachute," meaning you bail out of your job to be free to pursue your passion.

This is, of course, no easy decision. It's life changing, and I'm not suggesting it will be right for you. If your passion is meaningful enough and there's no place for it in your working life, you may have to consider yanking the ripcord. But there are several levels of action you can take, some less extreme. Let's look at each and review your options.

The Five Paths When Passion is Blocked

According to "career doctor" and career counseling columnist Dr. Randall S. Hansen, Ph.D., most people will change careers (not just jobs) several times over their lives. In this era of career plasticity and the Internet, it's rare for someone to stick with one life's work for fifty years. So if you're thinking about leaving, you're not alone.

But what are your options? In my experience, there are five paths you can walk when you're the person in charge and your passion is being met with everything from indifference to loathing. The right choice for you will depend on many factors: your age, your financial security, the type of people you work with, whether or not you have another skill set, and so on. Let's go through them.

Option #1: Leave for a different situation in the same profession.

Pull the plug. Hand in your resignation or sell your practice to someone else—perhaps a partner—and go off to start a new practice or business in the same industry. This is pretty extreme, but at least you're not leaving your profession. A perfect example of this is the physician I know whose small medical group had grown to a huge group over ten years, and then was bought by a major HMO. Not wanting to submit his patients to the red tape of an HMO, he left his group and started his own practice with three other doctors. Now he makes less money but enjoys his work much more. His financial profitability dropped, but his emotional and relationship stock *soared*.

To make this move, you need to develop your passion fundamentals: goals, core values, vision and so on. Then spend at least three months trying to engage your colleagues and employees on a passionate level. If you meet with little success, start asking questions. Can you transform your current situation to one that accommodates your passion without wrecking your business? Perhaps it's one person who's blocking your passion from taking hold, but that person is irreplaceable. Or is there hope for making gradual changes if you can be patient? *Can* you be patient?

I suggest an exercise in your Passion Journal: For one month, write your observations about your workplace in two categories: the obstacles to your passion, and the hopeful signs that you can bring about change. Track both for at least 30 days and see which column is longer. If you see more blockages than hope, leaving may indeed be your best option.

Keep in mind that this is not an unusual action. I've seen it many times: a doctor, lawyer, stockbroker or other professional starts off small, then grows too fast and too large for his or her liking. Ten years later, the business is riding its owner, instead of the other way around. Many experienced professionals choose to downsize—or "passion-size," as I like to call it—reinventing their professional environment to serve not only their customers, but their passions. It can be jarring for a short time, but it's usually deeply rewarding.

Option #2: Leave and do something different.

This is the Big One, the career equivalent of the lawyer's son who at age eighteen announces that he is not going to law school like the five generations before him, but instead going to Juilliard to learn to become a concert pianist.

Following this option means you've decided that it's not your office environment or personnel that are stifling your passion, but your profession. Honestly, few professionals follow this path before about age 60, when many finally have enough money in the bank to embark on that career making surfboards. Until that time, practical considerations usually carry too much weight. But my advice to you is, don't discount the idea of retiring from your current line of work and turning your passion into your job UNTIL you've explored the possibilities. There are many questions to ask:

- Is it possible that your dissatisfaction with your career is transitory?

- Could downsizing or changing personnel fix the problem?

- If you leave, could you sell your practice or business?

- How financially secure are you?

- Would retiring leave you with any potential legal liabilities?

Most important of all, can you turn your passion into a paying career? These days, thanks to the Internet, it's more possible than ever to take that thing you've always wanted to do and make a decent living at it. If you've always wanted to write a book and speak about it, the Internet is a fantastic tool. That's what I do for a living, and I can tell you, it's marvelous. So, based on your passion, values and goals, brainstorm on your passion and your current skill set. Is there a way you can combine them to turn your passion into a living while leveraging your decades of experience?

You might want to start your own business, become a consultant or indulge your creative side. Fantastic. How? Be creative. There are always ways to turn a passion into an income. For example, a friend of mine whose passion is organizing elaborate international vacations for his family decided to turn that into his profession. Now he consults with travelers and custom-builds trips for them, often learning about off-the-beaten-path places he'd like to travel in the process. That's what I'm talking about when I say, "Be creative." In fact, that's a Passion Principle:

> *Making a living from your passion*
> *will always require creative thinking.*

A worthwhile exercise if you're in this position is to start planning the steps you would take to exit stage right and leave your profession behind and land in the center of your passion. Make a list including these items and start brainstorming:

- How you would exit your profession organizationally and legally (personnel decisions, legal obligations, non-competes, etc.)

- How you would exit financially (selling, emergency savings, etc.)

- How you would develop your passion into a business

- How you would earn an income at your passion

- How you might combine your current skill set and your passion into a hybrid solution (legal experience and volunteering, for example)

Option #3: Transform your organization (stealth mode)

Here's your opportunity to get sneaky and have some fun doing it. Let's say that you decide it's not worth it to leave your professional situation for whatever reason. In that case, you need to transform that situation to make it passion-friendly, right? Well, there are two ways to do this: overtly and covertly. Here, we're talking about doing so in stealth mode, right under the noses of your staff and colleagues. It's challenging, but honestly, isn't that half the fun?

Transforming your organizational culture into one that is receptive to and supportive of passion is difficult to do without the cooperation of the other people involved, but it's not impossible. After all, you're the boss. You have access to every level of the business and the power to dictate change. But before you can know if an invisible passion campaign is to be waged, you should answer two questions:

1. Is your organization so change-resistant that a covert operation is in order?

2. Are there people you can trust to become your allies in this?

Alliances are especially vital. When I suggest you transform your organization in stealth mode, I'm not saying you can't share your plans with anybody. You simply don't share them with the majority of people affected. It's very useful to have a team of four or five people who understand your passion pursuit and can assist you in bringing about major changes in a quiet way.

When I talk about this approach, the most common question I hear is, "Why would I want to make changes without the cooperation of my people?" Many of my clients seem to think it's underhanded or devious. I disagree. It's your business, and by making the environment more amenable to your passion, you ensure that you'll enjoy your work more, do a better job, and be more successful. That's good for everybody from secretaries to partners.

The other answer to that question is that some people simply do not respond well to change. Such "change-resistant" individuals panic or feel threatened when they are forced into change. That can result in people quitting, poor customer service, unsafe conditions on the job, or a myriad of other problems. Faced with such potential for disaster, it's a smart professional that brings about change stealthily and avoids anxiety.

When you're launching a covert passion transformation, write down all the aspects of your working environment that need change and the level of change needed, ranging from "mild" to "moderate," "radical," and "reinvention." Then map out your strategies for introducing quiet changes to those areas. With this path, the key to success is *subtlety*. It's essential to weave in passion-centered changes gradually over time, so that people don't see the big picture until the changes have already occurred and they realize they *actually like things better* now. It's great when that happens. Covert transformation can involve steps like these:

- Slowly asking an employee to approach her responsibilities in new ways, introducing fresh methods a little at a time over weeks or months, always phrasing the redirection as a request and soliciting the employee's feedback.

- Gradually changing the physical environment in a series of steps—paint colors, new window coverings, new furnishings.

- Organizing regular staff events centered around activities that relate to your passion. For example, if you are passionate about vintage motorcycles, perhaps you could set up quarterly events for your people at vintage bike races, motorcycle shows or bike auctions, to give them a taste of what you love without stating it outright.

One of the best ways to maximize your odds of success in this effort is to try to encourage people to get involved, even when they don't know your larger purpose. Get their opinion on new décor for the office before you order, or ask them about how you could reorganize processes to make them more efficient. The more people who have "buy in," the easier the transformation will be. Above all, be patient. If you choose the covert method, you're committing to at least a year, maybe two, to bring about systemic change without freaking anybody out. So move gradually, not abruptly. And if someone calls you on the carpet and says, "What are you up to?" level with them.

Option #4: Transform your organization (open mode)

On the other hand, maybe you stink at keeping secrets. In that case, there's nothing wrong with coming out and stating that you're going to make some changes in the organization to bring it into alignment with your newfound passion. However, there are three things you must do to make this work:

- Tell everyone what your passion is and why it means so much to you.

- Encourage them to embrace their own passions.

- Ask for feedback, concerns, fears, ideas, etc.

In some ways, transformation in open mode is easier than

stealth mode. After all, you don't have to keep a secret. You can get ideas from your people that might turn out better than your own ideas. On the other hand, there are two big drawbacks. First of all, you may lose some folks who just don't handle change well. Second ... are you familiar with the phrase "too many chiefs and not enough Indians"? You may run into some people who want to take the bit in their teeth and do things their way, not your way. In that case, you'll need to make your vision clear and keep open lines of communication while leaving no doubt that *yours* is the final word, period.

Some of the signs that you can come out of the passion closet with your change ideas:

- Your people tend to be creative and iconoclastic.

- There's a lot of restless energy in your organization.

- People have told you they think things are stagnant.

- Your people have handled past change well.

You'll probably know if your organization is open to overt transformation. If it is, I have to confess that I prefer this path to stealth for an obvious reason: it makes the whole passion process collaborative and turns it into a joyous enterprise for everyone. If you can engage at least half your people in the process of planning, implementing and maintaining passion-centered change, you'll discover another wonderful Passion Principle:

> *The more people are involved in passionate action, the more they become inspired to discover their own passions.*

Option #5: Adjust your work to conform to an off-hours passion pursuit.

Let's say that it's just not realistic to transform your organization either quietly or loudly, and you're not going to leave. What can you do? I suggest this to a great number of my clients: modify your working arrangement to allow yourself more free time and energy to pursue your passion in your off-hours.

This is obviously the most conservative path of all, and the one most passion-centered professionals are likely to walk. It doesn't require earthshaking redirection of your life, just some adjustments. For instance, working one less hour three days a week, taking one day every other week off, or hiring a personal assistant to take care of the time-consuming jobs that you shouldn't really be doing.

The idea is simply to make more time for pursuing your passion when you're not working, and then jumping into your passion with both feet during your off-hours. Whether it's a hobby, the arts, mentoring, volunteering or anything else, start looking for an opportunity to engage in your passion that fits with your revised working life. A community college class that meets on your off day, for instance. There are always ways to make this work if you're creative. That brings up one more Passion Principle:

> *Passion demands that you rewrite the rules to benefit yourself.*

You've already proven that you're the kind of person who's willing to burn the rulebook just by reading this material. Keep going. You're only going to really live in your passion by not only defying other people's expectations of you, but your expectations of yourself.

Passion-Centered Leadership

Professional speaker and consultant Michelle Payn-Knoper says, "Leadership is passion. Without passion, a person will have very little influence as a leader. I believe passion provides an individual with the light of leadership and creates an undeniable drive to make a difference." I couldn't agree more. Great leaders are those who are able to inspire passion and purpose in others no matter what their jobs are. Done well, even a seemingly common job like administrative assistant becomes meaningful and takes on a transformative power. Great bosses don't lead by fear. They make people want to *become better*.

If you're the boss, you're already a leader to the people who work for you and with you. Your passion only increases the power and potential of your leadership. If you can bring the fire of your passion discovery to the office every day, it will become contagious. Everyone wants to be happy in what they do, to end the day feeling fulfilled and joyous. When the people who work under you see you exhibiting those qualities, they want to know why. You have the power to nurture their nascent passions, to help them grow, and to infuse your entire organization with the fire and possibility of passionate people. That's the ultimate transformation. That's how you become a genuinely passion-centered professional.

Tips and Tricks

These are some of the finest ideas I have seen used to exert passion-centered leadership. Feel free to try some or all of them, always keeping in mind that positive is better than negative, and that when you respect the input of others, you get them working for you instead of against you.

Create new "passion based" job titles. This seems insignificant, but it's really ingenious. What if you did away with "HR director" and "senior partner" and let people determine their own job titles based on what they love? You might have a "chief happiness officer" and a "financial research genius." That kind of small creative move can invigorate an office.

Hold passion meetings. If practically everyone in your organization is open about their passion, then it becomes child's play to hold monthly meetings where everyone talks about what they did in the last month to pursue their passion. People can talk about the classes they took, the crafts they built, the volunteer work they did, and so on. This can lead to people taking interest in getting involved in each other's passions—a sort of passion cross-pollination.

Encourage entrepreneurship. I'm not suggesting that you encourage your people to leave and start their own businesses. Entrepreneurship within an organization is a real thing. It means that you encourage your people to innovate, think creatively to solve problems and to "own" their ideas. They get credit for them, not some higher-ups. Develop a system to recognize and reward entrepreneurial thinking, and watch your people become more creative than you ever thought possible.

Create communication channels. Passions are never static, and the passions of your people will evolve over time. As they do, they will bring with them new challenges and ideas. Create multiple ways that employees can share with you their concerns or triumphs: an employee blog, a suggestion box, a private voice mail, a web forum and so on. Make some communication channels public and others private.

Find ways to make passion profitable. When the organization benefits, everybody wins. Search out ways to make passion benefit your bottom line. Encouraging entrepreneurship is a great way to do this, since innovation often makes things run more efficiently. But passion can also translate into superior customer service resulting in more referrals, or into people getting more done in less time, increasing productivity. Work with your people to think of ways their passions could increase revenues—and make it clear they will benefit financially.

Set passion policies. In fostering a passion-friendly environment, one crucial safeguard is setting rules that forbid people from stomping on one another's passion. As we've discussed, passions are as fragile as new-blown glass early on, and scorn or dismissal from one person can scuttle another's life mission. Set up guidelines for respecting and responding to others' confidences about their passions. Basically, no passion abuse allowed. If you don't think the other person's passion makes sense, thank him or her for sharing and excuse yourself. Nothing negative tolerated.

Get rid of the rules. This can be a tricky one, because it relies on an organization full of responsible veterans who can be trusted. But if you're lucky enough to have that kind of organization, consider doing away with employee manuals and such and letting your people make their own rules to serve their passions. They'll love it. The only caveat: work has to get done on time and with the same quality.

Allow employees to set business goals. Throw the doors to the inner sanctum open and let your staff chart the course for the organization—revenue targets, hiring, sales volume, growth, new locations, equipment purchases, etc. If they're passionate about the business, they will commit to making wise decisions, and they might do a better job than you would ever think. At the same time, you free yourself to do more of your work and pursue your passion.

Reward passionate performance. Finally, reward the people who show the greatest passion in their working life. I suggest something like a Passionate Employee of the Month or Year award. Recognize people who have shown an exemplary ability to blend personal passion and professional commitment. Make it a once-a-year lavish, gala event and make your people feel truly special and appreciated. They will make you successful beyond your wildest dreams.

That's all the advice I have for being a passion-centered boss. If you're not the boss, then you can still adapt some of these ideas for your own journey. Just remember, at the heart of every passionate professional is a person who wants to be respected and heard, and must grant others the same privilege. As long as you follow the previous steps and refine your passion and the driving values behind it, and live it honestly and fully, you can't go wrong.

Now, let's move along for a few final thoughts and ideas before I leave you to begin your thrilling passion journey!

Passion Principles from this chapter:

*Your position can also empower you
to pursue your passion.*

*Making a living from your passion
will always require creative thinking.*

*The more people are involved in
passionate action, the more they become
inspired to discover their own passions.*

*Passion demands that you rewrite the rules
to benefit yourself.*

Epilogue

If You Had Known Then What You Know Now...

*A man without passion is only a latent force, only a possibility,
like a stone waiting for the blow from the iron to give forth sparks.*
—Henri Frédéric Amiel

Passion has the capacity, as Shakespeare said, to overthrow reason. We should all be so lucky. But only a select few, a paltry number of our fellow sojourners, actually live in the core and flame of their passions, earn livings at them, and build their lives around them. You know them, and they're not necessarily wild-haired artists or writers (or speakers). They're anyone whose love for daily living radiates from them—people who know they're blessed and fortunate to spend their time on this earth doing something that means so much to them and brings so much joy to the world. That kind of person can be involved in any profession. It can be you.

Throughout *The Passion-Centered Person*, I have tried to walk you gently but decisively through the process of opening your eyes to your lifelong passion and reinventing your working life to center on it. Now the task falls to you. When you walk the passion path and discover your goals, your vision, your core values and your single focused passion, you will have gained the self-knowledge to truly integrate your passion into your work in a way that gives you joy and energizes your life. You see, this odyssey is not just about passion, but about your personal transformation. In the process of discovering your passion and opening your mind and heart to its power, you're changing for the better. It's inadvertent self-improvement. I'm sneaky that way.

A Matter of Humility

One of the comments I hear most often from my speaking audiences and my coaching clients is that they wished they had heard me speak about twenty years earlier. Well, twenty years ago I had not found my passion, so it would have been a boring speech. But in any case, I understand the feelings that this comment brings up. We all wish we had been wiser when we made life-altering decisions in our past. That's one of the ironies of living: when we have the freedom to choose our life's course in our twenties and thirties, we don't have the wisdom we have when we're in our fifties and sixties. Conversely, when we've gained the wisdom, we appear to be locked into a life path that's set in stone.

Note that I said "appear to be." As I hope I have made clear here, nothing is set in stone unless you're the stonemason. You always have the power to order change in your life—your career, finances, location, relationships. Yes, the older you get and the more static the conditions of your life become, the harder it is to change. But it's always possible.

Now, I'm a firm believer that people rarely change without crisis in their lives. It's human nature. Your discovery of your passion is a self-inflicted crisis of a positive kind. You know how a sudden heart attack will often motivate men to start exercising and eating right, assuming they survive? "Passion enlightenment" is an emotional heart attack that you will always survive, and it can have an even greater impact on your future. When your passion is so powerful that you simply MUST find a way to engage in it, you'll make titanic changes in your life, no matter how jarring they might be in the short run.

Another simple truth is that the pursuit of passion is a humble person's voyage. It requires admitting that you were wrong for not wanting more out of life. You need more than the degree, the title, the portfolio, the house and the car. No matter how old or young you are, you need purpose.

What Would You Change?

So if you had known back then what you know now, what would you change? What key decisions would you make differently? When people ask me that question, you know what I say? I tell them, "I wouldn't change a thing." It's a fool's game, and not for the reason you might think. I don't say that because it's impossible to change the past. In fact, some more recent research into physics actually shows that something called *retrocausality*, or the ability to influence the past, may be a real if paradoxical phenomenon. But that doesn't matter.

What I mean is that my journey, with its ups and downs and mistakes, put me in the right place at the right time to discover my passion, meet my co-author, and build my incredible life that has culminated in this book. You're the same way. If we could go back and change our errors, who knows if we'd end up at the same place? Would we have the wisdom to recognize passion when it spoke to us?

Where I believe this question can be helpful is in guiding you to the changes you want to make *today*. If there's a hobby or a career you wish you'd gone after in 1985, why not do it today? What goal have you always felt bad about not chasing? There's probably no good reason you can't go for the brass ring now. Instead of wishing you could go back in time and change your past, use it as a guide. Allow yourself to recall unfulfilled wishes from another point in time, then make them real. You'll know them. They are the ideas or life pursuits that give you butterflies and a pang of nostalgia (which literally means "pain of remembering"). For some people, they get that pain when they think about sailing their own yacht across the Pacific; others get it when they watch live theatre and wish they were on stage. Find that feeling and act on it. That's where your past can be a marvelous guide.

You Already Know This

This is one of the most profound ideas I want to share with you. You already know about your passion and what you need to pursue it. It's been inside you all your life. It's been speaking to you incessantly. But we in our modern lives, where the spiritual and philosophical has been discredited and driven underground by science and skepticism, are out of touch with our inner voices. We tune them out. We distract ourselves with work and consumption and politics so that we don't have to listen to our inner selves remind us of the opportunities we missed.

I'm not talking about religious doctrine. That can obscure inner knowing rather than assisting it. I'm talking about the purely spiritual inner awareness that comes from your connection to the universe. We've suppressed and silenced that voice within us, but that doesn't mean it's stopped speaking. We've just changed the channel —and we suffer because of it.

The inner knowledge that you have of what you're supposed to be doing is like a musical line. When you're listening to it, you're living in harmony, creating an accompanying music of your own that balances and complements the music. Life is beautiful and creative. You seem to spawn new ideas and inspiration wherever you go.

But when you're not listening, your life becomes dissonant. You're playing notes that just don't work with the music you're supposed to be living. If you're not aware of your passion, or if you've tuned it out because of life's pressures, you're still going to feel its effects. This isn't where you were supposed to end up. You don't know why you're not happy. Life doesn't seem to have any meaning.

Here's the great news: you can always open your ears to the music. You have always known about your passion—you have always known who and what you were meant to be. You can recapture that knowledge; it's never stopped trying to speak to you. All you have to do is hear it and listen. That's what this book is about: getting you to listen to the voice that's been inside you since you were a child. Once you can do this, you will be eager to make radical changes to the way you live your life.

What Now?

OK, that's enough deep chatter. What do you do with all this passion knowledge now that you have it? The first thing I suggest you do is think. By that I mean, take some time to think about your life and what it is today. Think about your past and the decisions you made that got you where you are today. Think about your motivations for making those decisions. Most importantly, think about the things you've always wanted to do and probably don't make much time for. Think about what you live for, as opposed to what you do to make a living.

The pursuit of passion depends on self-knowledge, so I would also suggest that you go out today and buy your Passion Journal, or create a computer file to write it. Make it private and secure, because no one else should be reading it. Then, just start writing down how you feel about what you're doing today and what you'd really love to be doing. Write down your fears about making changes, whether they involve losing money and going bankrupt or facing the unknown and the possibility of failure. Let yourself pipe-dream about your ideal life, whether it involves travel, art, sports or anything else. No editing, no disclaiming something as "stupid." There are no wrong answers in this test.

Do this for at least a few weeks. Then you're ready to take on the exercises I've given you in chapters four through eight. Start making your lists. Spend as much time as you need on your passions, goals, core values and the rest. You want to get this stuff right. If it takes you six months, fine. After all, you've been mucking about for how many years living in a way that doesn't make you happy, so what's a few months of good planning?

The other vital thing I suggest you do is to find an Accountability Coach as soon as you can. This can be a former mentor or teacher, a colleague or a family member. But it needs to be someone of uncommon wisdom who will call you on the carpet for your actions and never hold back in telling it like it is. Share your entire passion journey with your AC and ask him or her to be your reality check, the person who reminds you of the issues you haven't thought about or holds your feet to the fire when you make a promise to yourself and then fail to keep it. Think Mr. Miyagi from *The Karate Kid*, only with fewer punches and more unvarnished truth. I find that old college professors, gruff-but-gentle uncles and pastors can make fantastic Accountability Coaches.

My best advice: *begin the process*. When you get to the end of this book in a few pages, set it down and immediately start brainstorming your passion. Don't wait for your fire to cool. You've been hemming and hawing about this for decades, probably. It's time to make a change and have the life you know you deserve.

Quick Change Artist

The pursuit of passion can be a years-long chase, but it doesn't have to be an exercise in delayed gratification. You're not a monk, and you haven't taken a vow of chastity or poverty. There are some changes you can make in your life right now that will help you stay motivated over the long term and give you some quick reward for your new self-awareness.

- **Start a weblog.** Blogs are a genuine phenomenon. These simple online journals offer everyone from journalists and scientists to schmoes like me a place to write about their experiences and share their opinions. Why not start your own blog about your passion and your journey? It's a wonderful tool for writing any career poison out of your system and developing a running account of your passion journey. You can even use your blog as the venue for your passion exercises. You'll find fantastic free blog creation tools at blogspot.com, typepad.com and wordpress.com.

- **Take a class.** Some people will pooh-pooh the idea of taking a class as being a substitute for real action. I completely disagree. Taking a class—at a community college, the city or a private company—is a terrific way to get more acquainted with your passion and really fire up your interests. You might even meet people who share your passion.

- **Read about your passion.** Subscribe to magazines about your passion, buy books about it, find DVDs or TV shows about it. Immerse yourself in it. This is about giving yourself some short-term pleasure related to your passion as you begin the long journey toward bringing your passion into your profession. Only a fool undertakes a long journey without short breaks to enjoy the scenery. Reading magazines about what you love and letting your mind wander into daydreams about what life will be like is your scenic stop. Savor it and gain strength from it.

- **Meet others who share your passion.** Nothing is better than this. Blogging and classes can be ways to meet fellow passion voyagers, but another wonderful way to do this is Meetup.com. This fantastic website allows you to search for people who share your interests in your region and then meet them. You can also rely on everything from professional organizations to civic or fraternal groups. The goal is simple: find a "passion circle" of people who will support you in your quest as you support them. Let me tell you from experience that having help makes the journey not only easier, but more joyful!

Trust Yourself

I've spoken to accomplished dentists, lawyers, financial geniuses and award-winning architects—people with decades of experience at their demanding professions—who, when it came to the journey of passionate self-discovery, were as scared and helpless as toddlers. Or so they thought. What they really feared was failure. When you've been a wealthy, high-achieving professional for many years, you become accustomed to being master of the universe. It becomes easier to live with an unsatisfactory life than to risk seeking wisdom and passion and perhaps end up feeling silly or ignorant.

But as I said earlier, you already know this stuff. You have always known it. So as we come to the end of our time together, I ask you to do one thing: trust yourself. Even if you have zero experience in self-examination, or you feel silly talking about your passions after years of being completely pragmatic and grounded, you can do this. Remember the father in *Mary Poppins*? He was famously well-ordered and took pleasure in the rational predictability of his household—until he realized that his mania for work and order was denying him the joy of being a real father to his kids. Then he went and flew a kite. I'm asking you to remember what it was like to fly your own kite, then to get out and start flying.

Everything about the passion journey begins with asking questions, with holding your oldest assumptions up to the light and examining them to see if they are valid. Are you doing things because they are what you really want, or because they are expected of you? Are you staying in place because you're happy with where you are, or because fear of failure or embarrassment has paralyzed you? As I said, humility is required. Once we begin asking more and more probing questions of ourselves, we find out that not only are the answers not as bad as we feared, but that questions lead to more questions. In the end, we always come around to the only question that matters:

What is the meaning and purpose of my life?

When you're in your passion, you'll know the answer, and it will seem completely, foolishly obvious as you realize you've known the answer all along.

I want to leave you with one last notion. Perhaps you went after your passion years ago and failed. You couldn't make a living at it, or you didn't want to do the work. Perhaps you had to make a choice between the practical and the ideal and you chose the practical but uninspiring. *That does not matter now.* Know this: when you finally open your mind and heart to passion, you will always come back to it no matter how hard you try to avoid it. Even if you tried a career in music twenty years ago and bombed, that passion is still alive in you, waiting to be fanned into a flame. It's never too late to make your passion the center of your life. You never forget how. It's like riding a bike. The music is always there.

Make your passion and your profession one. You have the power. You've always had it. I wish you blessings and joy on your journey.

Made in the USA
Lexington, KY
27 September 2019